MINDFULNESS COLLECTION: 2-IN-1 BUNDLE

Power of Mindfulness Meditation
+
Mindful Path to Self-Compassion -
The #1 Complete Box Set
to Self-Acceptance and Self-Love
(Beginner's Guide)

THE POWER OF MINDFULNESS: CLEAR YOUR MIND AND BECOME STRESS FREE

Discover How to Live in the Moment Every Day. An Introduction to Meditation Practices Every Mindful Beginner Needs

Congratulations on purchasing Mindfulness Meditation:
A Practical Guide For Beginners, and thank you for doing so!

Every effort was made to ensure it is full of as much useful
information as possible. Please enjoy!

Table of Contents

Introduction

Congratulations on purchasing Mindfulness Meditation: A Practical Guide For Beginners and thank you for doing so. This book is all about using the power of your thoughts to be mindful and bring peace, purpose, and happiness to your life.

Drawing upon the rich tradition of Buddhism, mindfulness meditation is all about using your thoughts to be present in the moment and crafting the world that you want to live in. If you want to be more present in your daily life, this book is for you. If you want to heal and cope with chronic diseases, this book is for you. If you want to just sleep better or deal with your depression, then this book is definitely for you. Mindfulness meditation has been shown to have extraordinary effects on your life from your mental to physical health. This book will show you how to tap into the beautiful power of mindfulness meditation no matter if you are Buddhist or not.

The following chapters will discuss everything you need to know about embracing mindfulness meditation in your day-to-day life. However, an important distinction between mindfulness and meditation needs to be made before we proceed. Oftentimes, you see mindfulness and meditation used together. Other times, you may see mindfulness and meditations used interchangeably. Meditation is the more general term that refers to the practice of fine-tuning your mind through various mental exercises. Mindfulness is a form of meditation in which one focuses on being in the very moment compared to other types of meditation practices that may use chants or mantras. For the purposes of this book, it is important to note this distinction. Any meditation practice is great! However, this book will dwell on the importance of honing in on your breath with your mindfulness meditation practice.

Mindfulness Meditation: A Practical Guide For Beginners covers five chapters. In chapter 1, mindfulness meditation will be discussed thoroughly. How key concepts in mindfulness meditation relate to Buddhism, plus the benefits of mindfulness meditation, plus answers to frequently asked questions are included. The subject of chapter 2 is about how to practice mindfulness meditation. A practical guide about which positions are best and other best practices are highlighted. Chapter 3 explores more breathing and relaxation techniques that can be used to bolster your mindfulness meditation practice. The techniques in this chapter are able to help you vary your mindfulness meditation practice. Chapter 4 is dedicated to guided mindfulness meditation exercises that can help you as you begin your meditation practice. The scrips included will help you get started so you do not have to start your meditation practice from scratch. Chapter 5 is also dedicated to guided meditations, but the mindfulness meditation scripts in this chapter focus on guided meditations designed to heal various ailments.

This book about *Mindfulness and Meditation* will more than prepare you to begin your journey into mindfulness and meditation. There are a lot of famous people who practice mindfulness like Naomie Harris, Boris Johnson, Katy Perry, Richard Branson, and Anderson Cooper to name a few; thus, you are in great company.

There are plenty of books on this subject on the market, so thanks again for choosing this one! Every effort was made to ensure it is full of as much useful information as possible. Please enjoy!

Chapter 1: What is Mindfulness Meditation?

"To think in terms of either pessimism or optimism oversimplifies the truth. The problem is to see reality as it is."

– Thích Nhất Hạnh

How many times have we been encouraged to see the cup half full instead of half-empty? Oftentimes in western society, the push to be optimistic and to think positive is drilled into us from a young age. However, if one is beginning to become more mindful, the transition to mindfulness may feel a little jarring as it is opposite of what feels comfortable. Imagine this. Instead of focusing just on the positive aspect of life, mindfulness encourages a realistic outlook on life that embraces the good and the bad, the positive and the negative and the neutral. And this is where our book begins, starting off by learning about this effective way of living that has been used successfully for centuries – mindfulness meditation.

Buddhist monks have been using the power of mindfulness for over 2, 500 years. Mindfulness is the act of allowing your brain to rest while observing the thoughts that come and go in your mind. Mindfulness meditation is different from actively thinking and using your creative mind. When you are being mindful, you focus on an object, scene or sound that is calm and then let your thoughts gently amble by in your mind. Being mindful is powerful because if you are always caught up into being busy and always thinking about your next step, mindfulness gives you a much-needed break and makes you reflect on your pattern of thoughts and actions. It is the exact opposite of the daily living experience of most people because instead of going, mindfulness encourages you to slow down the pace.

Mindfulness allows you to know your thoughts instead of trying to change them. Instead of being judgmental and unkind to yourself if you think something negative, mindfulness has no judgment value on your thoughts. Your thoughts are just there. When you are mindful, you are taking notes of your thoughts like a note-taker. When you are in a mindful state, you just pay attention to what your thoughts are doing but giving them the freedom to do what they want. Ultimately, the goal of mindfulness is to know your mind. Once you begin to know your mind, you can begin the next step which is to train your mind.

The beautiful thing about our minds is that they are malleable, and as a result, they are trainable. Our minds are able to change based on what one is thinking. If you think the world is a horrible place, you will operate from a place of fear and your actions will show that. If you think that the world is a wonderful place, you will operate from a place of reckless optimism without being able to be realistic about certain dangers you may find yourself in. Mindfulness helps you to know your thoughts and then begin to train your thoughts to become more in tune with your long-term goals. Mindfulness slows down the grind of your busy daily pace and gives you a different vantage point about patterns in your life. These patterns can be feelings that you have in certain situations or your reactions to how other people treat you. When you are being mindful, you may notice trends and patterns that you are constantly thinking. Are you always wanting more and more? Do you feel comfortable with the way things are? Whatever patterns you notice, mindfulness can help you pinpoint what types of things are causing you mental, anguish, conflict, or joy. Then after noticing these patterns, you can begin to shape it to how you would like to be by focusing on being more gracious, compassionate, and kind with your thoughts.

When you begin your practice, do not treat your mindfulness meditation practices as an obligatory item on your daily to-do list. When you meditate, you want to be present in the moment, not treating the practice as an aggressive measuring stick to how fast you can change or using your meditation practice as a form of escapism without being willing to change your ideals. The most important thing to remember before you begin is that you are training your mind to be at peace with how things are going in the world, no matter what is happening. Once you are able to be at peace in no matter what situation you find yourself in, then you are able to start to work on yourself to change your values. Mindfulness meditation is not a sprint; it is a marathon that you continually work on until you are finally able to free yourself from unsavory emotions that are clinging to you whether they are anger, agitation, negativity, self-image issues, unfair, hasty judgments, and biased opinions and ideals.

When you are training your mind to be more mindful, affirmations are great tools to use. Affirmations are very helpful, especially when you create them yourself. The thought process behind using affirmations is to use very direct language which influences your subconscious to help you get the outcome that you want to get. When you use affirmations, you want to first figure out what outcome it is that you want. Then create a short sentence with an active word. Make sure the sentence is in the present tense. For example, if you want to feel calmer and not be so anxiety-ridden, you can create an affirmation to help. You will start with the outcome of being calmer and make that into a statement using the present tense. Thus, the affirmation would be 'I am more calm.' By using the present tense, you are affirming the future outcome. When the affirmation is created, you can say it during your meditation time and throughout the day. When you couple this practice of saying affirmations with your mindfulness meditation session, they work doubly together to help you get the outcome that you want to get. For example, you hear the term think positive all the time. It is because positive thinking can help shape your future to where you have a positive future. However, if you think negative oftentimes a reality reflects your thoughts. Our thoughts influence our subconscious which in turn can determine our reality.

Mindfulness meditation helps you shape your reality by taking the time to know your mind. Once you know your mind, you will be able to train it and ultimately free it from negative, debilitating thinking. Every step works together. Before you begin your mindfulness meditation practice, know that it is not going to be easy. It will be a journey, but if you are dedicated, you will see a difference in your life.

The History of Mindfulness Meditation

For Buddhists, nurturing mindfulness is the ultimate path to enlightenment. The point of Buddhism is to reach the highest truth by focusing on overcoming the limitations that your body has. Buddhists practice mindfulness by using four foundational truths of mindfulness. The four truths originate from a Buddhist sutta or sutra which is similar to a form of Buddhist scripture. The name of the sutta is called "The Discourse on the Establishing of Mindfulness" or the *Satipatthana sutta*. Please remember that the four establishments of mindfulness come from a very long and rich history. This book cannot possibly cover everything related to them, but hopes to serve as a general overview that can deepen your understanding of mindfulness meditation. The four truths are mindfulness of the body, mindfulness of feelings, mindfulness of consciousness and mindfulness of phenomena. Each foundation normally goes step-by-step in a flowing manner. You can go in and out of meditating upon each truth. They all work together. The first stop on the mindfulness journey is mindfulness of the body.

What is the one thing that you typically hear before beginning any form of meditation? The answer is watching your breath. Most meditation practices or guided meditations instruct you to begin by taking deep breaths in and exhaling deep breaths. Therefore, when you practice mindfulness, the first step is to think about mindfulness of your body. Initially, you'll want to start by being mindful of your breathing. Notice how deep or how shorts your breaths are when you start your meditation session. There are also different forms of body mindfulness you can focus on as well, such as mindfulness of eating or mindfulness of how you walk. These are some of the easiest mindfulness of the body to begin with, but we will focus on mindfulness of breathing since breathing is key to healing lots of ailments, physical and mental in your body.

Mindfulness of the body is just not about the positions your body is sitting in or how you breathe, eat and walk. Mindfulness of the body also involves a deeper understanding of how all your body parts work together. This includes how your leg connects to your thigh, how your ears function, or the power of body working throughout your body. Mindfulness of the body also seeks to understand some of the more unpleasant bodily functions such as urine or snot boogers or blood. The purpose of being mindful of your body is to reflect on how your body functions. You may ask, how do I try to be mindful of my body when I am meditating? An easy introductory way to do this is to imagine yourself greeting and thanking each body part for what it does. You can start at your feet and work your way up until you reach the top of your body.

The next foundation you should be concerned with when practicing mindfulness meditation is mindfulness of your feelings. A better way to explain mindfulness of your feelings is that this truth is concerned about being mindful of your neutral, painful, and pleasurable feelings. You can also reflect on how to be mindful of these feelings by using the senses of your touch, smell, hearing, seeing, taste, and your mind. In Buddhism, your mind is considered a sixth sense. It important to be mindful of these feelings because when you have painful feelings they can lead to fear and hatred. Too many neutral feelings can cause you to become disinterested and floated through life. When you are neutral about something, you are not concerned about it and as a result, it will not be important to you. Lastly, you have to be mindful of pleasurable feelings because too many pleasurable feelings can lead to lust and greed. It is important to be non-judgmental and only observe your thoughts, not acknowledge them when you meditate. The reason you do not want to acknowledge anything is that once you begin to acknowledge a thought as a neutral, painful or pleasurable feeling, you are in danger of attaching yourself to feelings that will prevent you from being enlightened. Thus, it is best to use mindfulness to observe when you are gaining feelings of neutrality, pleasure or painful so you know how to handle those feelings appropriately. When you practice mindfulness of feelings, you will still experience feelings.

Mindfulness of feelings does not mean that you do not feel. It only means that you are able to enjoy the feelings without going overboard to the point of the feelings cause you to become obsessed and overly attached to the thing that is causing the feeling, whether those feelings are good or bad. For example, if you love doughnuts and you find yourself obsessing over doughnuts, you can enjoy them so much that you want more and more doughnuts because of the pleasurable feeling that doughnuts give you. Eating too many doughnuts can cause issues your health like diabetes or chronic inflammation. All of these feelings started because of the seemingly innocent, yet pleasurable feeling of liking doughnuts. On the other side, if you are leery of a certain political leaning and it brings you immense pleasure, attaching yourself to that displeasure can quickly lead to hatred and biased feelings. However, if you are able to know your thoughts and know that this political leaning causes displeasure, you can work to be mindful that the political leaning is a trigger for you without attaching too much to that feeling to the point that it goes overboard. Likewise, if you feel neutral about a person, you can become so disinterested in them that you lose focus of the fact that they are human and worthy of respect. Hence, if they ever needed something, you would most likely overlook them or drag your feet to help them. So even feelings of neutrality can be dangerous. Once you become too attached to any type of feeling, the excess doting on the feeling prevents you from reaching enlightenment.

The next foundation of mindfulness meditation that you want to build upon is mindfulness of your consciousness. In Buddhism, there are 52 mental formations. Mental formations translated loosely are emotions and states of mind. The mental formations are normally grouped together in a specific way. The first of these formations are the previous feelings that were discussed in the mindfulness of feelings consisting of feelings of pleasure, neutrality, and displeasure. The next 51 formations are what the mindfulness of the consciousness helps you to focus on that are clustered in different groups. These include:

- Proficiency of mental properties

- Pliancy of mental properties

- Perception

- Composure of mind

- Appreciation

- Effort

- Righteousness of mind

- Worry

- Desire to do

- Amity

- Psychic life

- Error

- Perplexity

- Feeling

- Right livelihood

- Volition

- Initial application

- Attention

- Greed

- Buoyancy of mental properties

- Adaptability of mind

- Recklessness

- Right speech

- Sloth

- Discretion

- Proficiency of mind

- Modesty

- Conceit

- Right action

- Faith

- Buoyancy of mind

- Pliancy of mind

- Contact

- Deciding

- Concentration of mind

- Torpor

- Mindfulness

- Disinterestedness

- Envy

- Shamelessness

- Adaptability of mental properties

- Distraction

- Composure of mental properties

- Dullness

- Balance of mind

- Sustained application

- Pity

- Selfishness

- Reason

- Righteousness of mental properties

- Hate

This is a general overview of the mental formations, but you can study them in more detail to get a more detailed understanding. To simplify this foundation, when you are practicing mindfulness of the conscience, be observant of the different feelings that go in and out of your brain. To easily start meditating with mindfulness of the conscience, when you meditate observe any thoughts that you have. When your mind drifts from focusing on your breathing, you can call out to yourself that you are being mindful. When your mind begins to drift from not meditating, you can call out to yourself that you are not being mindful. This simple exercise is using mindful of your consciousness. It is also a great trick to use in your everyday life when you want to be more mindful.

The last foundation of mindfulness that you want to build upon is mindfulness of phenomena or mindfulness of perception. When you think of a car, you know it is an object that has four wheels and has the capacity to take you here and there. The idea that you have in your mind of a car may be realistic and based on a car that you know personally. Or the idea of a car that you may have can be based on what your perception of what a car is generally, according to your knowledge of what a car is. When you practice mindfulness of mental objects, you try to focus on the 'why' of how you perceive something. If you think of cars as positive, this positive association could be because of a childhood memory that when growing up you had a wonderful experience of your parents taking you to school every day in an old beat up, yet comfortable car. If you have a negative perception of cars, it could be because your friend was killed by a car or cars cause you to think of all the damage that they do to the ozone layer. Mindfulness of perception allows you to focus on the experiences that shape your perception of what something is so you can bypass those perceptions to get to the true meaning of what something actually is and not what you think something is.

When you practice mindfulness of perception, you want to be aware of things that can cause your perception to be tainted. These can be known as the 5 hindrances. You also want to be mindful of the 7 factors of awakening which should be what you aspire your perceptions to be based on. When all of these factors work together, it helps you eliminate suffering. The 7 factors of awakening that you want to focus on when you practice mindfulness of perception include:

- Equanimity – This factor can be described as the calm observance of things around you.

17

- Energy – This is the energy that powers you to lead the investigation to seek understanding about different topics in life.
- Concentration – The complete focus of the mind is what this factor seeks.
- Investigation of your perception – This factor encourages you to seek knowledge about phenomena to understand how something operates.
- Joy -Balanced pleasurable interest in something is what this factor is all about.
- Tranquility – Serenity and quietness encompass this factor.
- Mindfulness – Present moment awareness describes this factor.

The 5 hindrances to avoid are:

- Dullness – Doing your takes half-heartedly with no vim or lacking concentration.
- Lust – A craving for pleasure to fulfill all your senses.
- Ill will – Feelings of hatred directed to others.
- Restlessness and worry – This is when you are unable to calm your mind.
- Doubt – A lack of trust or conviction.

When you monitor your thoughts to see if any of the 5 hindrances appear in your train of thoughts, you want to note when and why they arose. You'll also want to note how you can prevent the hindrance from appearing again and how you can replace the hindrance with one of the 7 factors of awakening in their wake.

As you work on your mindfulness meditation, strive to attain the four foundational truths in the order of mindfulness of body, mindfulness of feelings, mindfulness of consciousness, and mindfulness of perception. This is ideal. However, you can meditate upon all of the foundations in one setting as well. So, if you focus on more than one truth at a time, that is ok as well.

To truly attain enlightenment, you must find a way to master them all.

Lastly, mindfulness meditation helps you cultivate awareness of the "three characteristics of experience." According to Buddhism, if you do not understand these three characteristics, then you are bound to be caught up into an endless cycle of suffering. The three characteristics you should be aware of are the traits of impermanence, or *anitya*, dissatisfaction, or *duhkha*, and egolessness, or *anatma*. Impermanence means that all conditioned things will change. There is a constant change that you must be aware of. The next trait of dissatisfaction means that there is pain and suffering and no satisfaction in an unenlightened state. *Anatma* means that one should strive to act without an ego. These three are another aspect of Buddhist underpinnings behind the mindfulness meditation practice. These are great to keep in the back up your mind when you are doing mindfulness meditation.

Hopefully, up until this point, the case for why you practice mindfulness has been made. In case you still are not convinced, let's try to convince you one more time. So why mindfulness? There are lots of different meditation practices you can choose from, but mindfulness meditation is a great way to begin for a few different reasons.

Mindfulness is awesome because it:
- Helps you not be judgmental – One of the major components of mindfulness is to not be judgmental of yourself and others. This gentleness towards yourself improves your overall self-esteem. It also encourages self-compassion for yourself and for others.
- Easy and fast – There is no set time to do it. It is super easy to pick up on and relatively fast to do. Your sessions can be as long as they need to be or as short as they can be. If you have a busy schedule, you can meditate for 5 minutes or however long is best for you.
- Reduces stress instantly -Because the necessity of breathing is at the core of mindfulness meditation, deep

breathing immediately reduces the stress you may be feeling as soon as you begin your mindfulness meditation session.

- Improves your wisdom – Mindfulness meditation improves your wisdom because you are able to figure out what makes you tick by noting and understanding the power of your thoughts. You also are able to be wise about other people, because this system meditation improves your observation skills such that you will be able to observe others and make connections about their behavior in ways that you have not been able to before.
- No set way to do it – For some people, the fact there is no set structure may be limiting to them, but it is a positive because there is not a right or wrong way to do it.
- Relaxing and calms your nerves – Just like reducing your stress instantly, mindfulness meditation also relaxes and calms your nerves due to the power of breathing.
- Observe yourself in the moment – Mindfulness meditation allows you to be in tune with your thoughts and actions so you are able to get into the 'zone' a lot easier than before.
- Easy to pick-up – Did I mention how easy mindfulness meditation is to pick up? Once you have one session, you will be able to do more rather easily.
- Doesn't have to depend on anyone else to do it – Mindfulness meditation is great to practice on your own. So you never have to worry about if the teacher is going to show up to class or not. This meditation style is self-guided so you can set your schedule according to your convenience.

There are also tons of researched and proven health benefits from doing mindfulness meditation. Mindfulness meditation is a factor in:

- Managing pain that's chronic – Mindfulness helps you strengthen your focus so you are able to focus on other things so that you can manage your paint.

- Reducing anxiety, stress, and depression -Again, the breath and it is healing power makes mindfulness meditation phenomenal at relieving issues with stress, depression, and anxiety. People who practice mindfulness meditation regularly oftentimes have lower blood pressure and a stronger immune system.
- Helps you sleep better -The relaxation that comes from mindfulness meditation helps you hone in on your triggers that help you sleep. It is a surefire sleep aid.
- Helps elderly and pregnant women – Mindfulness meditation does a great job of helping elderly people not feel so alone, anyone for that matter, and it is also a great labor tool for pregnant women.
- Improves intuition and creativity – Mindfulness meditation is a favorite of creatives and helps improve the creativity in non-creatives, too.

While there are lots of Buddhists background informing mindfulness meditation, you do not have to practice Buddhism in order to practice mindfulness meditation. This is a common misconception. Do not fret. You may have many more questions, and the chapter will end by clearing up common misconceptions one may have about mindfulness meditation.

I have trouble clearing my mind when I meditate. Is it a necessity that when I meditate for my mind to be completely clear?

No, having a completely clear mind is not a necessity before you begin to meditate. Mindfulness meditation helps you to see your thoughts more clearly. Your thoughts are supposed to trickle along in your mind instead of racing by. Think of mindfulness meditation as allowing your thoughts to go by like a weather scan. They can change minute by minute or hour by hour. Your meditation practice allows you to be in tune with your thoughts. It allows you to keep a pulse on how your thoughts change.

I'm not good at yoga. Will I still be able to do mindfulness meditation?

Sure thing! Mindfulness meditation encourages people to get in a comfortable position before they meditate. For some that may be a popular yoga pose like the lotus pose, but that is not a requirement. Other lie down or sit in a comfortable position. Whatever is the most comfortable position for you is the position that you should use. Also, while mindfulness meditation encourages you to be still, there are lots of moving meditation like yoga or tai chi or mindfulness of walking that encourages movement while you meditate if you ever want to build on your mindfulness meditation practice.

Will mindfulness meditation clear all my problems instantly?

Great question. Mindfulness meditation is not a quick fix. Its power lies in the ability to locate thought patterns and behaviors that may be problematic for you. If you have certain health problems, mindfulness meditation is a great way to cope, but if your symptoms continue to persist, you may need to check in with a doctor for further suggestions for treatment. Mindfulness meditation may not totally eliminate your stress, anxiety or depression, but it will help you cope and manage the situation a lot better than if you were not meditating and certainly without the use of medication.

Is mindfulness only for those who practice a certain religion?

No. You can be any religion and practice mindfulness meditation. It does draw from the Buddhist tradition, but just because you practice mindfulness does not make you a Buddhist, just like drinking wine does not make you a Christian. The great thing about mindfulness meditation is that it can fit in your lifestyle no matter if you are religious or not. If you are interested in adding more Buddhist elements to your practice, feel free to learn more and incorporate it into your mindfulness meditation journey.

Is not mindfulness just dealing with positive thinking?

Mindfulness meditation encourages non-judgmental positive thinking when examining your thoughts, but it does not run away from negative thoughts. Mindfulness meditation also encourages the examination of neutral feelings as well. When you meditate and negative thoughts occur, it is encouraged that you examine the thought and try to figure out where it came from and why you think that way as a way to be able to handle any situation you may find yourself in, whether that situation is positive or negative.

How long will it take me to learn mindfulness meditation?

The journey to learn how to meditation has no set schedule. Learning how to do mindfulness meditation can actually be quite linear. One day you may do well and feel like you're moving forward, yet another day, you may feel like you are going nowhere. One day you will be able to do all the exercises correctly, and the next day you may run into trouble. It is more important to be consistent when you meditate so you can feel comfortable and improve your practice for you to receive the benefits.

To recap, this chapter focuses on the history of mindfulness meditation, which has been utilized by Buddhist monks in the last 2,500 years. The good thing is, you do not have to be Buddhist to practice mindfulness. It couples well will any lifestyle. Mindfulness meditation is built on four foundation truths including mindfulness of the body, mindfulness of the conscience, mindfulness of feelings, and mindfulness of phenomena. A major component of being mindful is being in the moment. Like any skill, it can be learned and improved upon with more practice. Since we have looked into detail about what mindfulness meditation is, now let's get started! Chapter 2 walks you through the first step before your first mindfulness meditation setting.

Chapter 2: Getting Started with Mindfulness Meditation

"When we get too caught up in the busyness of the world, we lose connection with one another – and ourselves." – Jack Kornfield

How often does it feel like life is racing by? We often do not have the time to take the time and smell the roses. We often do not take the time to truly embrace our loved ones just to hug without feeling like we have to rush off to the next thing. In this social media frenzy of a world we live in today, it is easy to lose focus. As a result, if we are not careful, we can easily move like a zombie in our day-to-day lives without fully experiencing everyday life. Thankfully, when you begin to practice mindfulness for just a few moments per day, you will find that you will become more open to the full experiences of life and our daily activities will slow down. And we may, shall I daresay, begin to enjoy life for yourself and enjoy thriving relationships with others to the point that life becomes enjoyable. Yes, mindfulness meditation is a seriously powerful tool that can change your life, but it is also fun! And guess what the fun part is?

The fun part about being a mindfulness meditation practitioner is actually doing mindfulness meditation. Before you begin to meditate, a few ground rules need to be set. Also, a few things should be given as a reminder, too. First thing, when you are being mindful, remember that you are being mindful about something in the present time. The second thing is that for our practice, we will be using our breaths as the center of mindfulness. The more you become aware of what is going on around you and are able to use your breaths to center you, the easier you will be able to experience mindfulness. Becoming mindful can help you break through any biased perceptions you may have, and it may make you feel uncomfortable at times. However, if you are able to make it through the discomfort, you will be able to enjoy it fully. Also, remember, mindfulness does not judge your thoughts or focus on any bias that you may have. It just notes your thoughts as they pass by in your mind until you are able to just let the thoughts be. Your thoughts are not good or bad. You are merely a video recording nothing that you see. Mindfulness helps you experience real-time in super sharp focus. The more you dedicate to focusing on being mindful, the more your mindfulness muscle will be developed, and the easier doing mindfulness meditation will become

The very first thing you should do before practicing mindfulness meditation is to set a pin in your busy schedule that's going to be dedicated to your meditation practice. This is very important. When you set this time, please be consistent. Make sure that this time is distraction free with no person or task able to distract or interrupt you. If you need to set an alarm to remind you, do so. If you need to set your phone on do not disturb, do so. It is important for you to take this seriously if you want to get good at it. To help you set yourself up for success, stick to the time you want and do not let anything get in your way.

When you first begin, it is normal that you may feel a bit weird. Hence, to help you acclimate to the process faster, try to meditate more than one time per day. You can try to have a meditation session at least two times a day. To help make the transition easier, you can try to meditate at the same time every day, but if you aren't able to do that it is okay. Worst-case scenario: on that day you want to meditate, but you are unable to, try to make up the time that you missed. If you absolutely have no time to spare in your super-jam-packed schedule, you can try to meditate while doing another activity. If this is the route you must take, when you are doing the other activity, focus on doing the activity and make note of the thoughts that pass through your mind while you are meditating. For example, you can try to meditate while cooking. When you meditate while doing an activity, make sure that you are doing the activity for its value, not for some other end. For example, if you are cooking, you are cooking because the cooking is an activity, not because you begrudgingly have to cook for your family. Another time people like to meditate is while driving, especially if they have a long commute. Just be careful not to get too relaxed that you lose focus behind the wheel!

Another way to ease into your meditation practice is if you start off meditating in 5-10 minutes increments, at least twice a day, then work to increase your time. If you are having a difficult time even with the 5-10 minutes, you can start off by dedicating just 60 seconds a day and build from there. If you find the 60 seconds challenging, cut it down to 30 seconds and build from there. I cannot stress the importance of whatever you select, commit to it, because if you are able to commit at least 11 days of meditation, your mindfulness meditation habit is more likely to stick than if you did not do at least 11 days.

Something else to consider before you set your time is to consider the time of day that you want to meditate. For some, doing an early morning session sets the tone for the rest of your day. If they can meditate in the morning, they find that the rest of their day goes smoothly. They experience less anxiety and frustration. They remain calm and peaceful throughout the day. For others, the best time to meditate is not in the morning, but the reverse time. Some find that when they mediate after a long day of work, they can decompress from the day's stress and be set up to begin a brand-new day. When they meditate at night, they can sleep better because they are more relaxed and have put their stress to the side. Others still prefer to meditate in the mid-day. This allows them to settle down from the hustle bustle of the day and then prepare them to finish the rest of the day out strong. They also find that a quick afternoon meditation session reinvigorates them and gives them a much-needed energy boost in a much healthier way than eating sugar or drinking caffeine. Not to mention they do not experience any crashes either. I suggest trying every time to see which time is better. If you want to take your practice to the next level, commit to meditating at least twice a day to see how that affects you.

The second step you want to do before you begin meditating is to find the place where you will be meditating. When you find the place, hook it up or customize the place to your liking. For greater comfort while meditating, you can consider purchasing a meditation pillow to sit on or lie on. If you want to save money, you can use what you have around the house, like comfy pillows that you already have around. You can use a comfortable blanket or shaggy rug, as well. Once you select your place, you will also want to make sure that the place is free of distractions. If there is a computer or television or tablet or phone nearby, be sure to put it out of your sight so you cannot be distracted by it. If there is a place to plug your phone in nearby, do not charge your phone in your meditation place. I guarantee you that when you begin to meditate your phone will become a huge distraction. The saying 'Out of sight, out of mind' is definitely true! When you are selecting your room, consider the placement of the room in relation to your house and outside. You want the room to be quiet. There's nothing more distracting than trying to meditate and you have a huge noise to overcome, like an ambulance or fire truck passing in the background. Sometimes it is impossible to eliminate noise completely but try to eliminate as much noise as you can. In your meditation room, make sure that the room temperature is comfortable for you. You do not want it too hot that you're uncomfortable and sweating or too hot that it makes you groggy. You also do not want the room temperature too cold that you are unable to move your fingers and toes.

Once you have your time selected, and your special place decorated to your liking, it is time to meditate. On the day that you want to meditate, you want to figure out the best position that you want to be in throughout the session. One of the most popular poses is called the lotus pose. It is an advanced yoga pose and requires some flexibility. It is the one pose you most often see people in when they are meditating. Before you begin, you will want to stretch. To get into lotus pose, you'll want to be seated on the floor and have your spine straight. Let your arms rest by your side. Then you will want to bend your right knee and bring it to your chest. Then, drop your right ankle on the crease in your left hip so your right foot sole is facing the sky. The top of your foot should be resting on your hip crease. Next, do the same thing on the other side. Bend your left knee and put your left ankle on top of your right shin so your left ankle is crossed over the top of your right shin. Your left foot sole should also be facing upwards and the top of your ankle and foot should be resting on your right hip crease.

Once you are in this position, bring your knees into your body as close as possible while sitting as straight as possible. Your groin should also be as flat and close to the ground as possible. You'll want to put your hands on your knees with your palms facing up. Then create a circle with your thumb and index finger and leave the rest of your fingers extended. Lotus pose can be challenging for those with limited flexibility or those who are just beginning to yoga. The good thing is that there are other positions you can try using if Lotus Pose is a challenge for you. You are able to sit on the floor with your knees bent and legs crossed over each other. You can also just sit in a chair or lie down. The most important thing is to find a position that is comfortable for you.

Once your time is selected, your space is ready, and your position is selected, it is time to begin meditating. When you are in the most comfortable position possible, try to let your body feel loose. You can do this by rolling your neck and arms and shoulders in a circle. You can also stretch the muscles in your face by making a full smile and then a half smile. As you get loose, if you have any tension feel it roll away. Next, you'll want to make sure that your posture is top-notch. Keep your back and neck as straight as possible. Try to keep your stomach relaxed. To take your posture up another level, you can tilt your chin down slightly. Using the correct postures will allow your breaths to be as deep as possible and you will be able to draw in deeper breaths. After your posture is checked, you can then figure out what to do with your hands if you are not doing lotus pose. Your hands can rest on top of your lap, to the side of you on the floor or on top of one another on your knees with your palms up. The next decision you have to make is to decide what to do with your eyes. You can decide to keep them open, half-closed or closed completely. If you decide to keep them closed, be sure not to fall asleep when you are meditating. If you are afraid you may fall asleep, it may be best to keep your eyes open or at least half-open.

Next, focus on your breathing. First, just observe your breath. Remember, breathing is the key to helping you concentrate throughout the meditation exercise. As you breathe, you can notice your chest going up and down. Breathe in through your nose and exhale through your mouth. It is totally ok to breathe through your mouth if you have to. Once you have observed your breath, you can then begin to count your breaths. When you breathe in through your nose and then exhale through your mouth, count it as one breath cycle. Try to count to 5, which would be five completed breath cycles of inhaling an exhaling. Then try to get to 10 with your breath cycles. It should go like this: Inhale-one. Exhale - two. Inhale – three. Exhale- four. If any thought interrupts you, start the count over again until you are able to reach 10 complete breath cycles. This is a wonderful breathing exercise to do when you begin. Now remember, you are just starting so it may be difficult to retain your concentration and that's ok. Be patient, kind and gentle with yourself. If you do find yourself losing focus, the most important thing is to get back on focus as soon as you lose focus by concentrating on your breaths. Keep practicing this until you are able to count to 10 breath cycles with ease.

Then the next step to take your breathing to the next level is to begin counting your inhales and exhales as 1 complete breath cycle. It would look like this: Inhale – one. Exhale – one. Inhale – two. Exhale – two, and so on and so forth until you are able to reach 10 with ease. Once you are able to do that, then you can begin to focus on your breath only. This may take a while, and that's ok. You also may have trouble completing focusing on your breath, and that's ok as well. If you have a thought to interrupt your concentration on your breathing, observe the thought and then begin to count again. The easier you are able to control your breath, the easier your mindfulness meditation will be. Then you can start meditating while doing other activities until mindfulness just become of your daily life.

So, what happens if you are unable to still your mind? That's ok. Keep practicing until you get better. What happens if you are unable to sit in the lotus position? That's ok as well. Find the most comfortable position for you and then go from there. What is I'm unable to be nonjudgmental with thoughts that arise? Guess what? This will take time as well. As long as you are dedicated to improving your meditation practice every time you do it, you are making progress. The more you do it the easier it will be. This is a lifelong commitment so do not feel like you have to be perfect starting out.

This chapter has given you a wide overview of how to get started with mindfulness meditation. As a recap, before you begin your mindfulness meditation practice, make sure that you have already committed to a consistent time that you will meditate in order to build your practice. Try to start off at least five minutes twice a day for at least 11 days so you can build a habit. Once your time is selected, you will want to make sure your special meditation place is specific to you and your needs and most importantly, free of all distractions. There are a variety of positions you can take when meditating, just be sure to choose one that is most comfortable for you, whether it be lotus pose, sitting down, lying down, or standing. When you do begin to meditate, focus on your breathing. Be non-judgmental about thoughts that may float by. If you do find yourself being distracted, bring your attention back to your breathing. More importantly, be gentle with yourself and remember that the more you practice, the better you will become. The next chapter will focus on more detailed breathing and relaxation techniques that can help improve your mindfulness meditation practice.

Chapter 3: Breathing and Relaxation Exercises

"There is something wonderfully bold and liberating about saying yes to our entire imperfect and messy life." – Tara Brach

Let's face it. Life is not pretty. As a matter-of-fact, sometimes life can get downright ugly. Bills are always due, every two weeks. Relationships aren't always going as planned. And sometimes we just don't like ourselves. On the flip side, there are times where we can feel like we are soaring above the sky with happiness. There are times when we can do no wrong and it feels like life is going exactly as planned. However, the beauty in life is the embrace of both the good and the bad and the neutral. No matter what situations may happen to us in life, we can also count on our breathing and mindfulness to make the most of it.

Since the basics of mindfulness meditation were covered in Chapter 2, it is now cover breathing and relaxation tips that can help bolster your mindfulness meditation practice. As you nail down the basics of your breathing that were covered in the previous chapter, the exercises in this chapter will help you vary the breathing methods you use in your meditation session. The purpose of this chapter is to bring for all the different types of breathing and relax methods you can use to better your mindfulness meditation practice. This chapter will begin by exploring breathing techniques, some used in the yoga meditation tradition, and then will switch focus to relaxations techniques which will bring the chapter to a close.

In yoga, the Sanskrit word *pranayama* means breath. If you practice yoga or if you do not, then you must understand that at the core of both activities is breathing. Steady, deep breathing centers the practitioner in yoga and in mindfulness meditation. In this chapter, seven yoga breathing techniques that will be examined that can help you with your breathing in your mindfulness meditation sessions. As you listen about each one, take notes or memorize about which ones you would like to incorporate into your meditation sessions. The more you try, the more varied and fun your practice will be.

The first breathing technique is called Lion's Breath. It is an easy and fun breathing exercise to do. It does require you to be rather loud, so make sure that you warn the people around you if necessary. To begin, you'll want to be in your comfortable position. You can either be sitting in a chair, in lotus pose or lying down. When you're comfortable, inhale as deeply as you can through your nose. Then lift your arms up with your hands extended and breathe out loudly through your mouth, like a roar. When you breathe out, make the 'haa' sign like you trying to fog up a car window. You can also stick your tongue out when you exhale, too. Lion's breath is a great breathing exercise to relieve tension in your mouth and jaw. It also helps stimulate the muscles in your throat.

The next breathing exercise you want to try out is a popular meditation breathing exercise. It is known as 'bee breath' or *bhramari ranayama*. For this exercise, you need to be in your comfortable position and put your fingertips on your temple. Next, breathe in deeply from your diaphragm and when you exhale out, hum loudly like a 'humming bee.' Do this for a minimum of three breath cycles. This exercise is very helpful at getting your concentration back when you are having trouble focusing. And it is fun, too.

The name of the next exercise is called 'bellows breath.' It is great breathing exercise to do when you need a boost of energy. You also need to be loud for this breathing exercise, so be in a space where it is ok to be loud. To begin, make sure you are comfortable in your space. Then you want to raise your hands in the air like small fists. When your hands are in the air, you can spread your fingers out, too. Next, breathe in deeply through your mouth and every time you exhale bring your elbows close to your body and make a 'HA' sound from your diaphragm. This exercise should be done at a minimum of 3 breath cycles for as many times that you would like.

The 'breath of fire' is the next breathing exercise. This breathing exercise is great for bringing warmth to your body as well as detoxing your body. Just like any other breathing exercise, you want to begin by being in your comfortable position. You want your arms to be resting comfortably by your side. Once you are set, take a deep breath through your nose. When you exhale, instead of exhaling through your mouth, you want to exhale through your nose. But instead of a regular exhale, pump your exhales out through your nose in short sports and pull in your stomach while you do. Do the exhale quickly and make sure that when you inhale again, the exhales match your inhales in time, depth, and force. A similar breathing exercise to this one is called the 'skull cleanser.' It also raises your energy levels. Get comfortable first. This time when you breathe in, instead of putting your elbows to your sides, raise your arms up when you exhale. You still want your inhales and exhales to be done in short spurts, as well as, making sure that the inhales and inhales match in time, depth and force.

The next breathing exercise is one of the most common breathing techniques called the *ujjayi* breath. Before you begin, be in a comfortable position. You will then inhale by using your nose and then exhale by using your nose. However, when you inhale, you want the breath to drag at the back of your throat like you are drinking a beverage with a straw so that a hissing sound is made. You want to extend both your inhales and exhales out until both your inhales and exhales are deeper and smooth as possible. Start the exercise with a deep inhale and let each breath cycle deepen in intensity.

Kumbhaka is the next breathing exercise and its purpose is to help you retain your breath so you can perform deeper inhales. This breathing exercise focuses on the space between an inhale and exhale when you breathe. When you breathe in your nose and then exhale out of your nose pause before you take the next breath cycle. When you inhale, try to keep the breath at two counts, when you exhale, try to exhale at two counts and then when you hold your breath in between the next breath, hold your breath for two counts. After you do this one time, do a regular inhale and then exhale. Then try to do the breath cycle again when you hold your breath after you complete one breath cycle. This exercise can be combined with the *ujjayi* breath in the previous paragraph. *Kumbhaka* is a great warm up before you get deep into a mindfulness meditation session because it helps you set the tones for deeper inhales.

Now we are going to focus on breathing exercises that are not specific to the yoga meditation tradition. The first technique is called left and right nostril breathing. This technique is interesting because, at any time, we inhale and exhale through one nostril more times than the other nostril. This pattern changes every 90 to 150 minutes. Our nostrils are connected to opposite sites of our brains, so our left nostril is connected to our right nostril and the right nostril is connected to the left side of the brain. This technique is great breathing exercise, but it also helps you deal with qualities associated with the particular nostril. For example, the left nostril connects to the right side of the brain is associated with sensitivity, synthesis, calmness, empathy, receptive and cleansing energy. The right nostril connects to the left side of the brain and is associated with concentration, vim, willpower, gumption, alertness, warmth and nurturing energy. To do the exercise, you want to put your right thumb over your right nostril and then inhale solely through your left nostril. Then take your ring finger and put it over the left nostril so you can exhale out of the right nostril. Then keep your fingers there to inhale in your right nostril, then switch fingers and cover the right nostril so you can exhale out your left nostril. Then repeat on each site. This exercise can be tricky so be careful to take note of which nostril you are inhaling and exhaling out of to prevent confusion. This exercise is great for helping you to gain clarity and sharpen your discipline skills.

Equal breathing is another important foundational breathing exercise to know. We've already covered it somewhat but did not mention the specific name. For equal breathing, you get comfortable and then inhale through your nose for 3 counts and then exhale from your nose for a minimum of 3 counts. The important part of equal breathing is to remember to inhale the same number of counts on every inhale and inhale. You can do more than 3 counts of breathing, just make sure that you do the same count on each side. Abdominal breathing or diaphragmatic breathing is at the crux of your breathing exercises. It is also called deep breathing, and it is simply a deep breath that draws from your diaphragm rather than your chest. If it feels weird to breathe from your diaphragm, you should practice diaphragmatic breathing. This method helps your inhales get deeper. You can also put one hand on your chest and another hand on your ribcage to make your breathing deeper. Doing this allows you to feel your breath going in and going out. This breathing technique also helps prevent you from breathing through your chest only. By breathing through your diaphragm is improves your lung and digestive functions, too.

The next awesome breathing exercise is called 4:7:8 breathing. This exercise is similar to the *kumbhaka* breathing exercises that we have named before. For the 4-7-8 breathing exercise, you get comfortable. Then begin by exhaling through your mouth and try to make a 'whoosh' sound. Next, you will need to begin to inhale through your mouth. Close your mouth from the previous exhale and when you inhale, hold the inhaled breath for at least to the count of four which you will count in your mind. Next, hold your breath for 7 seconds. If you are initially unable to start at 7 seconds, that's ok. Hold your breath for as long as possible. Then exhale again, but this time make the 'whoosh' sound to the count of eight in your mind. You can make the breath slow and steady so it can last to the full eight counts. The entire sequence is considered one breath. It is best to start slow with this exercise then increase the speed. When you begin, try to keep the 4:7:8 count as close as possible so you can nail the correct breathing technique.

Since we've discussed breathing exercises, now it is time to begin discussing relaxation exercises. Relaxation is important because it helps heal your anxiety and depression. It improves your skin and your heartbeat and breathing which in turn improves your overall reaction to chronic stress. Without proper rest and relaxation, your body begins to break down because you have no way to rejuvenate yourself. While you may be good at the breathing exercises, your brain may still have racing thoughts. By coupling the relaxation methods with your breathing exercises, you are able to add another layer of stillness to your meditation practice which will make you more aware and present in the moment.

The first relaxation exercise is called autogenic relaxation. The concept behind autogenic relaxation is that you have everything your body needs to relax. (Autogenic means self-regulation or self-generated.) With this method, you visualize that your body is warm and relaxed. The autogenic relaxation method is great for stabilizing your heartbeat, relaxing your entire body and helping you achieve deep breathing. The method is easy. You first begin by finding a nice comfortable place to relax. Then you mentally work your way through visualizing warmth or calmness coming to every part of your body. The warm and calm feeling helps you feel relaxed like you are in a cozy blanket. Begin from the top of your body and work your way down or begin at the bottom of your body and work your way up.

For example, when doing at autogenic exercise (going from the top of your body to the bottom of your body), you begin by feeling relaxed in your head. You can imagine that your head is experiencing a wonderful burst of calm and loving warmth. Then imagine that the feeling of warmth has made its way to your forehead area. You can feel the warmth cause your forehead to tingle and melt all your tension away. Next, you'll want to follow the warm feeling all the way down to your stomach area. Repeat to yourself that your stomach is warm. Then feel the warmth travel down your legs, thighs, shins, and toes, warming every part until you get to the bottom of your feet.

While doing this type of exercise, you can also turn your attention to your breathing at any time. Note how calm and energy-giving your breaths are. You can also focus on your heartbeat and note how steady your heartbeat. It is also great to feel how your heartbeat sends warmth and relaxation throughout the rest of your body, especially your extremities like your arms and legs. Other phrases (or variations thereof) you can say while doing an autogenic meditation are that 'I feel relaxed.' or 'My body feels calm and quiet and comfortable.' or even 'I feel the warmth radiating throughout my body which relaxes and calms me.' (These are a few phrases that can help you get started.) Once you finish, imagine yourself doing an activity that you love. Whether that is relaxing on the beach or playing on the playground with your inner child. The ending activity can even draw on a dear memory that made you feel loved, safe or confident. The ending thought is a comfortable way to transition from the total feeling of relaxation of the autogenic exercise back to your day-to-day life.

The visualization technique is the next form of mental exercise that you can use to relax. This exercise is also fun to do because it requires that you use your imagination. Do you remember when you were a kid and you always used your imagination? It seems like the use of imagination gets lost the older we become. However, with this visualization exercise, you're able to tap into your imagination part of your brain and go back to using your imagination like in your childhood days. A visualization meditation session is similar to daydreaming in that you think of images that may you feel happy. However, visualization is active and present in helping you figure out how to relax your body by using your senses to think of imagery that helps you relax. Normally, daydreaming usually takes into account memories that make you feel good, whereas, a visualization exercise would observe a negative memory, make note of it, and then return back to the more pleasant feeling. A visualization exercise is also different from a guided meditation because you are in charge of finding the memories of what you're most comfortable with instead of relying on the guided meditation to help you visualize images that help you relax. Lastly, and distinctly, a visualization meditation exercise draws upon all of your senses of touch, taste, seeing, hearing and smelling to visualize the most relaxing moments to so that you can experience a state of relaxation for your entire body.

To begin a visualization exercise, you first must find a comfortable position in your special place. Once you are comfortable, think of an image that makes you feel warm and relaxed. This image can be of you walking on the beach. You can imagine the warm wind whipping at your hair or the warm sun extending its warmth over your body. You can smell the fresh scent of the ocean spray and accidentally taste the salty spray of the ocean as you dip into a way. You can hear seagulls loudly cawing in the turquoise blue sky while the gritty sand can be between your toes. While you are visualizing, do not forget to breathe deeply. You can inhale through your nose and exhale through your mouth. After you finish one visual image, you can transition into a different one. Do not feel like you have to stick to one visualization throughout your meditation session. You can transition back and forth between different imagery.

For example, after visualizing a peaceful beach scene, you can transition to a visual image of you sitting at a holiday dinner table surrounded by family members and friends that you love. The scents of your favorite foods fill the air. Foods like freshly baked bread, cheesy macaroni and cheese, roasted chicken and your favorite desserts fill the air. You can even smell the scents of your favorite person, whether it's leathery, fruity or more flowery. What other scents do you smell? After you work through one sense, like smell, you'll work through all the rest of the senses. How does the food taste when you eat it? Do your taste buds explode from goodness? Does the air taste warm from the heat in the kitchen? How does your clothing feel against you? Are you wearing your favorite blouse or shirt? Are you wearing jeans or some other type of material? Visualize the tight embrace from your grandma or parents. And what about the sounds? How loud is your aunt and uncle's laughter? Imagine the gentle cry of a newborn recently born into the family. How about the holiday playlist playing your favorite songs? Or imagine the lacy detail of the holiday tablecloth. What does the overall scene look like? Who are you sitting next to at the table? If you do not sit at a table, how is the seating arranged? You can be as detailed as you would like as you go through the scene in order to get as many great memories during your visualization session. You can also go as fast as you would like or as slow as you like. Choose to end the visualization on a very happy memory and feel how relaxes your body is. Then take a deep breath and open your eyes so you can go about your day. This exercise is very helpful in helping you relax, and it is one of my favorite relaxation methods to use. You can also couple a visualization meditation session with the use of with affirmations, especially if you already have a list of affirmations written. For example, after each image you visualize, you can say to yourself, 'I am relaxed.'; 'I am calm.' or 'I am happy.' after seeing it. You can also use your affirmations to visualize an outcome that you would like. If you are trying to reach a goal, you can visualize what it looks like when you reach the goal. Use all your senses to imagine the scene and use your affirmations after each scene as well.

For example, if you have a goal of receiving a promotion, you can do a visualization session of you receiving the promotion. Imagine how your boss' office will look like when you get the promotion. How does the office smell? What are you going to smell like? Will you have your favorite scent on? What will you eat for breakfast that day? Will your palms be sweaty? What will your celebration party look like? How will your friends, family, and coworkers act? After each image, say an affirmation, like, 'I work hard, and I am worthy of a promotion.' 'I can do anything I put my mind to.' to name a few. Remember, the more detailed you are, the more helpful the session is. This is a powerful tool to have in your meditation arsenal.

The last relaxation technique examined in this chapter is called progressive relaxation. Progressive relaxation is also known as body scan meditation. The technique behind progressive relaxation is to relieve your anxiety levels, too. This method of relaxation is powerful because when your body is physically relaxed you cannot be anxious. If you are experiencing an anxiety attack or feeling anxious, by the end of a progressive relaxation session, your anxiety should be gone, and your body should be completely relaxed. If you have chronic anxiety, this tool helps you relieve the anxiety outside of using medication. This method is also great at helping relieve chronic pain because it helps you relax and take the focus off the pain. Progressive relaxation involves a simple two-step process. First, you tense the muscle group that you are working on and then you let the tension out by relaxing the muscles. You will then take notice of how the relaxed state feels which helps you relax easier the more you do this method. You can either begin at the bottom of your body and then you work up or you can begin at the top of your body and work your way down. Before you start, make sure that you are in a comfortable position lying down on your back. Then you can begin.

- With your first muscle group or body part, breathe in, and tense the first muscle group (Tense firmly, but not to the point of pain or cramping.) for about 4 to 10 seconds. Be mindful that you do not tense too hard and cause pain which defeats the purpose of the exercise
- Then breathe out and completely relax the muscle group as quickly as you can (do not relax it gradually).
- Keep the muscle group or body part in the relaxed state for about 10 to 20 seconds before you work on the next muscle group.
- Notice the difference between how the muscles feel when they are tense and how they feel when they are relaxed. The relaxed state is helpful to know so if you ever needed to relax without doing this body scan, your muscle memory can kick in.

- When you are finished with all of the muscle groups, count backward from 5 to 1 to bring your focus back to the present.

The great thing about this technique is you do not have to be tense in order to practice it. It is best to practice it when you are calm so when you are anxious you are able to go through the steps without being confused since you've already practiced it. The body map you can follow when doing the body scan can look like this. You can start on one side and do one side completely and then go to the other side of your body. You can also do both sides at the same time before progressing to the next side of your body. This example body scan goes from the bottom of your body to the top of your body, by doing one side at a time.

- Feet - Wiggle your toes and point them to your face. Then point your toes downward. If you feel any tension from the waist down when you do this, relax your body.
- Lower foot and leg - Make your calf muscles tense by pointing your toes towards you.
- Thighs - Squeeze them hard and then let them go.
- Entire leg -Squeeze your thighs again and note any tension you may experience. Release the tension.
- Glutes - Squeeze your butt together and then release them.
- Hips - Roll your hips around and then let them go.
- Stomach - Hold your stomach in and then let it go.
- Back - Arch your stomach away from where you are resting and then bring it back down.
- Chest - Take a very deep breath for 5 to 15 seconds.
- Hand - Close your fist as tightly as possible and then let it go.
- Upper arms and biceps - Squeeze your fingers into a fist, bend your arm at your elbow and then flex your bicep in the muscle formation.
- Forearms and wrists - Extend them and bend your hands back at your wrist.

- Shoulders - Perform a shrug. Try to bring your shoulders as high as possible, aim for your ear, and let the shrug go.
- Front of the neck - Move your chin downward and try not to cause tension in your head and neck when you do it.
- Back of the neck - Press your head into the floor as far back as possible.
- Your mouth and the area around your mouth - Purse your lips as tightly as possible.
- Jaws and cheeks - Smile the widest smile that you can.
- Around the bridge of your nose and eyes - Wiggle your nose and then close your eyes as tightly as possible.
- Forehead - Frown as deeply as possible and wrinkle your forehead while you do so.

Once you finish going to the top on one side and make it to your forehead, you can go back down throughout the rest of your body. Once you are great at practicing the entire body, you can make the exercise shorter by doing a shorter version that focuses on the main body parts. You can also pick and choose what body parts you would like to scan so you can create your own customized progressive scan. A shortened body scan example would look like this:

- Lower limbs (legs and feet) – Point your toes upward, tense your calves and squeeze your thighs on both sides.
- Stomach and chest – Breathe in and breathe out as deeply as possible and feel your stomach contract as far as possible.
- Shoulders, arms, neck – Raise your shoulders up high as possible and let them go. You can flex your biceps and then bend your wrists as far back as possible. Be sure to do this on both sides of your body.
- Face – Wrinkle your forehead and the area around your nose. Smile as widely as possible and frown as widely as possible to work your entire face.

After becoming a pro at knowing how your body feels when it is relaxed. You can then focus on the relaxed or released part only. You can do the full body by relaxing or the shortened body. Initially, the release only technique may feel different as it will feel less intense than the full tense and release exercise, but the more you practice, the more you feel comfortable with the full exercise.

Great job working through this chapter! Hopefully, you've made plenty of notes and highlighted the exercises you want to try. This chapter highlighted all the ways that you can use breathing and relaxation exercises to add to your mindfulness meditation practice. The breathing exercises draw from some popular yoga breathing exercises like lion's breath, *kumbhakam, ujjayi,* and bee breath, spirit of fire, and bellows breath to name a few. Some breathing exercises also include popular breathing techniques such as equal breathing, 4:7:8 breathing, and left and right nostril breathing. Popular relaxation methods covered in the chapter are autogenic relaxation, progressive relaxation, and visualization techniques. The next two chapters will focus on specific mindfulness meditation scripts that you can use to help you start your mindfulness meditations and to diversify your meditation practice.

Chapter 4: Mindfulness Meditation Exercises

"A mind set in its ways is wasted." – Eric Schmidt

When was the last time that you tried to learn something new? Maybe you had to try out a new recipe or take a new way to work? Perhaps you have to try a brand-new form of communication that was drastically different from what you have already tried when communicating. Whatever it is that you had to learn, I'm sure that it was not the easiest thing. However, once you finally learned what to do, how awesome was the feeling to know that you accomplished something? As you start off with meditating, it may be a little rocky at first, but keep going! You will learn how to get better. And that's when the real run begins.

So, it is time to take the fun up a notch. The next two chapters are dedicated to giving you guided mindfulness meditation exercises that you can practice on your own. Before you begin, do not forget to be in the most comfortable place possible in your meditation place. You can lie down, be in lotus pose, sit or stand up. If you are sitting, try to have your back and posture as straight as possible. If you are lying down, let your arms and hands rest loosely beside you without having any tension in them. You can also decide to have the lights on or lights off. You can also decide if you want to keep your eyes open, closed or half-open. It can be very relaxing while you meditate, so make sure that having your eyes closed will not cause you to go to sleep! Remember, breathing is at the core of your exercises. So as you listen, remember to breathe in and breathe out. If at any point, you feel that your concentration is beginning to shift, firmly and quickly bring your attention back to your breath and to the meditation script.

Basic Mindfulness Meditation (Short)

Before you begin, be in the most comfortable position for you. You can dim the lights or keep them on. You can open or close your eyes, whatever is most comfortable. As you begin, try to slide into a calm state by relaxing your thoughts. Inhale to three counts and then exhale for three counts. Imagine your body receiving the life force of oxygen bringing energy to every part of your body that your breath touches.

If your thoughts are speeding by, try to slow them down and just watch them as they pass. As you see each one of them pass by, put them in a box. Inhale deeply through your diaphragm and exhale through your mouth. Feel the breath tickle your throat as the tension is exhaled out.

Whatever is upsetting you or whatever is making you happy, release those thoughts from any judgment you may have. Observe them as they are without trying to fix your problems, looking for solutions or wishing the problems will go away. Watch your thoughts glide by in your mind until they are gone. Bring your attention back to your breath. Breathe in deeply and then breathe out through your mouth.

Be aware of what your mind is thinking but try not to focus in on them to the point that you are not breathing deeply. Remember to breathe in deeply from your diaphragm. Lengthen your shallow breathing with your deep breaths. Notice the calm that the deep breathing brings to your body. Breathe in through your nose for a count of five, 1, 2, 3, 4, 5, and let the breath out through your mouth for a count of five, 1, 2, 3, 4, 5. Feel the breath rippling through your body as you breathe in again. Then let the breath go back out.

When you breathe in through your nose this time, take in as much air as you can possibly manage. Feel the breath powering you and just be. Be still. Be in the moment. Embrace the physical sensations around you. If you're sitting on a fluffy rug, feel the rug. Feel the material of your clothes rub against your skin. Feel the arms on your hair tingle.

Inhale and feel your chest move gently up. Then exhale and feel your chest move down. Exhale until it feels like your back is touching the floor. Feel the power that deep breathing has on your entire body.

Inhale and exhale through your mouth. Make a gentle whoosh as the breath leaves your body. Stay calm and relaxed. If you find yourself losing focus, do not beat yourself up. Be gentle and kind to yourself. Bring your focus right back to your breathing. Breathe. Hold your breath for a count of 5 seconds. Exhale for a count of 5 seconds. And let that breath out for 3 seconds. When you breathe in, feel your entire body relaxing with the force of the breath that you breathe in.

Wiggle your fingers, your toes, your nose, and your eyes. Feel the skin wrinkle and smooth once you return your body back to its resting position. Inhale deeply and be in the moment. Exhale deeply and be in the moment.

Feel the presence of your being. Reward yourself for taking the time to be mindful. Be grateful that you have the chance to be still and take in this very moment, not the past, not the future, not one minute from now, just the very present moment. Breathe gently in and out. Do not feel like you have something else to do or you need to rush this moment. No. Indulge in the presence of yourself and the universe. You are a wonderful being that is able to fully appreciate this moment through your breath.

Your inhales and exhales anchor you to the present time and give your appreciation for being able to be still. Breathe in this time hold your inhale for at least 10 seconds. Let go and exhale for another 5 Seconds. If you are not able to inhale for at least 10 seconds, that's okay. Inhale for as much as you can. Exhale.

Center your focus back on the moment and prepare yourself to bring yourself back to your critical mind. Prepare your moment for embracing the present time and every second that it brings, whether good or bad. Open your eyes and welcome the light.

Try to keep this state of mindfulness as you move throughout the intensity of the day.

Basic Mindfulness Meditation (Long)

Find the most comfortable spot for your body to rest, whether that is lying down, standing up, or sitting. If you have on any tight clothes, loosen them so your body can feel free and unrestricted. You can turn off the lights in your room or close your eyes. If you are at risk of going to sleep, keep your eyes half-closed.

Breathe in and then exhale. Shed any judgment that you may have on thoughts that are passing by. Instead of thinking of your thoughts as criminals that must stand before you, the judge, do not mete out any punishment for the thoughts that you think. Merely let them skate by like a pair of young kids on roller skates. Inhale and use your deep breaths to steadily slow those thoughts down. The more air you take in the slower those breaths are.

Exhale all the tension out of your body for a count of four, 1, 2, 3 and 4. Then hold your breath for 7 seconds. 1, 2, 3, 4, 5, 6, and 7. Then breathe in for a count of 8: 1, 2, 3, 4, 5, 6, 7 and 8. Wonderful.

Breathe in deeply until you feel your heart rate slow. Breathe out deeply until you feel your heartbeat at a steady pace. Notice the thoughts that you feel. And let them be. You just be, as well. Let only your breathing connect your body to this present moment in time. Do not think about tomorrow. Do not think about what you're going to do after this recording. Do not think about what you did before this recording. Focus only on your breathing and being still.

If it is easier for you, exhale and open your mouth wildly. Exhale all of your expectations and items on your to-do list. Exhale all the anxiety and unpleasantness you may feel. When you inhale, breathe and feel the pleasure of just being. Feel the calmness taking over your body. Breathe in the importance of being able to be still and know that everything is going to be okay. Feel any tingling or sensations you may have. If you feel numb, or any discomfort, slightly shift your body until you are comfortable again.

Then close your eyes, and if you feel the flutter of your eyes against your eyelids, be grateful for that. Know that your body is simply floating in this moment in time. Instead of trying to anchor your body with heavy thoughts, let it simply be. You and your body are perfect as is. Reward yourself for being mindful by taking in a deep gulp of air. Then let out all the heavy burdens that are weighing you down through your breath. Breathe in again.

Imagine that relaxation is wrapping your entire body like a magical carpet. Your deep inhales power the carpet, and your deep exhales keep the carpet floating. If you find that your mind is wandering, bring those thoughts back to focus by focusing on your breath. Do not judge yourself if you're having trouble focusing initially. Commend yourself for trying. Remember you will continue to get better with time. Always bring the attention back to your breath.

Slightly feel the 'whoosh' of the breath leaving your nostrils and tickling your nose hairs. Welcome that breath back into your body by breathing deep from within the walls of your stomach. Feel that breath traveling through your stomach, up to your chest, up to your head, and returning back down, straight down to your feet. Exhale and breathe in and then feel the breath travel throughout every bone in your spine and throughout every finger back through your mouth.

Do that one more time. Take a deep breath from the pit of your diaphragm. Then exhale the air back out into the world just as deeply as you took the breath in. Great job.

Breathe in deeply and feel the breath traveling throughout every orifice of your body giving you energy, confidence, and gratefulness for being able to reflect on this moment. When you exhale, exhale those intentions good or bad that you are having. Do not feel the need to be industrious. Do not feel the need to be so awful to yourself.

Enjoy this moment to refresh by concentrating on your breathing. Take another deep breath and hold it for as long as you can. Exhale that breath for as long as you can. Breathing one more time and then open your eyes.

Wiggle your fingers and toes. Feel the force of energy move into your wrists and back into your hands. On the count of three open your eyes: 1, 2, 3.

Take the mindfulness with you throughout every moment of your day. Know that anytime you need to be mindful, you are armed with a tool that can help you remain calm and happy and mindful by using your breath. Feel free to use this tool at any time throughout your day.

Breathing Meditation (Short)

For this breathing meditation, we will focus on your breathing. This 5-minute breathing exercise is perfect for those on the go. This exercise is intended to help you focus on your breathing while replenishing your body with the energizing mentally clarifying power of your breath. You can lie down or stand up or sit whatever is most comfortable for you. Before you begin, make sure that you are in a comfortable position with the lights dimmed. Feel loose by tensing your fingers and your toes and letting them go. Do that one more time. Point your toes as far as they can to your head. Then relax your toes and let your toes go back to a comfortable position.

Now that you're in your comfortable position, take one deep breath in. Feel your stomach draw in like it is touching your spine. Feel your stomach get as flat as possible. Lift your head up and breathe out. Breathe out all the bad thoughts and negativity that may be pent up. Feel the power of the breath circulating throughout your body. Feel the air touch every part of your body and bringing energy and positive vibes.

For the next breath sequence, we're going to try a lion's breath. Gently make sure that your hands are lying to your side of your body. Let them stay there resting without feeling like you have to move them. If they are clenched, unclench them and let them feel loose. Feel the calmness of your hands and let that feeling transpose on to your body. This time when you breathe in, breathe in as deeply as you can. Breathe in with your mouth closed. Then open your mouth and let the breath out like a lion roar. It is okay to make a loud sound. Stick your tongue out to get all of the air out of your esophagus. Close your mouth.

For this breath sequence, do a seven-count inhale. Breathe in for 7 seconds: 1, 2, 3, 4, 5, 6, 7. Then exhale for eight counts: 1, 2, 3, 4, 5, 6, 7, 8. What a wonderful deep and full breath sequence. Feel how calm and smooth and relaxed your entire body feels. Feel how light your body feels. Breathe in again.

There are no thoughts about today, tomorrow, or even the future that is bogging you down. Relish this lightness. Remember this feeling of relaxation. Let's try another deep 4:7:8 breath sequence. Making sure that you are breathing deeply, place your hand on your stomach and breathe in deeply. Feel your hand draw back as close to your body as your stomach is drawing in as much breath as you can. Exhale for 4 seconds: 1, 2, 3, 4. Hold your breath for seven seconds. Then imagine you are a gas tank. Take as much air in as possible. then hold your breath for 7 seconds: 1, 2, 3, 4, 5, 6, 7.

Now just like air is coming out the balloon, open your mouth and exhale all of that air out. Feel the relaxed feeling that's rocking your body. Feel how good it feels. Be aware of your breath only. Imagine that when you are just being, you radiate a beautiful color. It can be your favorite color. The more you are being and the calmer you are, the more vibrant your body radiates.

Breathe in deeply again and exhale just as deeply again. We will be ending the meditation soon so gently stir your mindful mind.

Slightly come back to this moment of critical awareness. When you get back to your critical mind, feel the necessity to be mindful throughout the rest of your day.

On the count of three, open your eyes and gently lift up. You can slowly stand and pack yourself on the back for completing a great breathing exercise. One. Two. Three.

Awareness of Breath Practice

For this exercise, awareness of your breath is the object. Please begin by feeling comfortable in a safe special place. Be in a dignified position whether that is lying down, sitting down, or in Lotus Pose. Just for a few moments, give way to your breathing and feel your breath coursing throughout your entire body. Replace all the tension and anxiety and shallow breathing in your body, with total complete relaxation and deep breathing. Feel your body responding to the deep breaths. Feel how your heartbeat slows. Notice how the tension removes from your body with every breath. Once you are there, imagine what your relaxed body feels like. Feel your body going limp like a noodle but not a soggy noodle, and al dente noodle. Feel soft and relaxed, yet firm. Hang loose and comfortable. Let all the tension leave your body.

Allow your breaths to rule the moment. In this present moment, you want to let your thoughts wander delicately around your brain. Let them bounce gently around the walls of your mind. Instead of your thoughts bouncing quickly and rapidly, let them bounce smoothly and steadily. Observe what the thoughts are. Once you observe the thought, imagine that they disappear with a soft poof. Let the thoughts leave and just be. Still your brain again.

In the meantime, give all the attention to your breath. You want to breathe in deeply through your nose. Feel the breath enter your nostrils and down your throat. When you exhale, exhale through your mouth and feel the breath leave your tongue and your teeth and makes it back into the world outside of you. Feel what your body feels like when it is just still. Your body is warm and empty and open. With every breath that you feel, imagine the oxygen in your bloodstream sending energy to every part of your body.

When you inhale notice how freeing it feels. Notice how the oxygen replaces any negativity that may be in your body. Instead of focusing on negative thoughts, have no judgment. Your thoughts are just that. If you're having positive thoughts, have no judgment on those thoughts. Just let them be. Focus on the breath Breathe in gently but deeply and exhale just as deeply. If you want to make a soft sound with your inhales and your exhales, that's fine. If you would like to try a huge lion's breath at this time, feel free to do so. Take a deep breath in and then exhale the breath out. When you exhale, let yourself exhale with an audible 'aah' like your own personal roar.

Feel how empowering that feels. Feel how wonderful it is to let out all of your anxiety in tension in your personal lion roar. Try it one more time.

Breathe in for a count of five: 1, 2, 3, 4, 5. Then let out your personal roar one more time for the count of five: 1, 2, 3, 4, 5. Stick your tongue out this time when you exhale. Feel your heartbeat, and calm it down by taking in one huge breath. Then you can let it out. Breathe in and feel how your body reacts. Breathe out and feel how your body reacts. Notice how your body feels between each breath.

Next, we are going to try a bellows breath. This will speed up your heart rate and then we will slow it back down.

Breathe in. Breathe out. Make each breath that you breathe in the same length and depth as the breath that you breathe out.

We will do this four more times.

Breathe in. Breathe out. Hold your breath for three counts. One. Two. Three.

Breathe in deeply from your diaphragm, then breathe out for the same count length until your stomach is as flat as it can be. Great job.

If you feel distracted at all, move the thought to the side. Let it disappear and bring your attention and focus back to your breath. We have two more bellow breaths.

Inhale. Then exhale.

Breathe in and breathe out. Hold the breath. Good job. Now breathe deeply and smoothly. Feel how awesome our breathing is. What a wonderful tool is it. See how wonderful is can change our heartbeats or moods with the simple sustenance of air and good breathing.

The breaths are bolstering your present breath. If you're comfortable in your position, think of a nice gentle breeze blowing right over your body. Feel comfortable being in this moment. You do not have to think about the worries of today, tomorrow, or the future. You're simply feeling comfortable and still. See the clouds floating above in the sky. Look at all the delightful shapes they are making, gradually, smoothly, and changing.

Whatever thoughts you're having that may make you lose focus, gently wipe them to the side. Hear the wash of the waves against the shore relaxing your body. Imagine the warm temperature rocking you to a state of relaxation. Feel at peace with the noise of fun around you on each side of the beach. See a small crab walking by your beach chair. Stay calm and watch it pass. Instead of holding your breath, breathe in deeply and slowly until the crab passes. Enjoy the warmth of the sun warming you.

Relax your body to the point that you feel like you're about to enter a deep sleep, but you're aware of everything around you. Feel the breath tugging your throat as you breathe gently and fully. Feel your lungs expanding. Taking as much breath as you can. Hold it there. Let the breast bubble out and give power all throughout your body. Breathe out make a slight 'O' with your mouth until all the breath is out. Feel like a balloon with no air left in it.

Once your breath is out, inhale again and gently awaken your senses. Feel your body arriving back into your critical space. You can slowly turn the switch back on to the grind, but this time, instead of moving so fast, take a step a little bit slower. Be a little bit more mindful when you are doing your usual activities in your day to day living. We will bring the meditation to a close soon. However, do not feel any pressure to end soon. If you would like to continue being mindful for a few more moments, that's ok. When you are ready to end the meditation, you can gently open your eyes.

Once your eyes are open, you can stand and have a wonderful day. Take the state of relaxation with you throughout the rest of your day.

Breathscape Practice

For this session, you will be guided through a meditation session that uses your breath as is the main focus of awareness. Before we begin, please spend time fixing your body in a comfortable position. If you are sitting, try to keep your spine as straight as possible, stick your check out, and have your head up. Let your head be balanced squarely between your shoulders, and let your gaze rest softly and gently as a point in space or a point on the wall. If it is more comfortable, you can close your eyes. Allow your hands and arms to rest in the position that is most comfortable for you. Do not let them feel heavy. Let them feel loose and light.

Before we go any further, turn off the switch to your daily grind. For the next few moments, no thinking about what types of things you need to do. No thinking of what someone said to you that pissed you off. No thinking of what you didn't get done to do. Please turn on the switch to your mindfulness mode. You are allowing yourself to stop for a moment and delight in this mindfulness. This switch only allows you to focus on what's going on in the present moment. Your mindfulness switch is only kind to your thoughts. You are no longer judgmental of what you think. You are only watching the thoughts as they go by. Now you are only aware of what's happening in this present moment. As you sit in a comfortable position, be still and feel. Feel the small hum of your breath as your chest moves up and down. Enjoy all the physical sensations that come with just being. Imagine that you are the epitome of what it means to be a bump on a log.

Be aware of how your stomach moves while breathing and exhaling. Feel how the air travels through your nostrils and then feel the slight lift of your shoulders and in your chest. Observe your breath cycle especially where it feels the strongest. When you feel that you are getting the most air, how does it feel? At one point do you feel like you are getting the most air? Is it when your stomach is drawn in as you feel your chest with air, or does your breath cycle feel the strongest when the breath comes in through your nostrils? Travel with your breath from when it comes through your nose, goes to your lungs, and pushes out your stomach slightly. Feel how the breath goes out of your body.

Observe the in-between movement of your breath. Notice the in-between time of when your breath comes in and when your breath goes out. Think of the entire sequence of breathing in and breathing out as one complete breath cycle. Notice how every part of your breath cycle is special, and it helps bring life into you. Focus on the moment in between your breath cycles. Try to even it out and make it the same depth, length and intensity as your inhales and exhale.

Inhale. Exhale. Space in between. Inhale. Exhale. Space in between.

While you focus on your breaths, you may experience your mind traveling. You may think about what happened last night or what you need to do after this or what you did before this session or something that's bothering you. Allow those thoughts to sashay right out of your mind. Bring your attention back to your breaths as gently as possible. Feel your breath and the sensations it provides as it travels throughout your body. Be aware of how your mind can easily go from one thing to one thing and bring it back to focus on your breathing. I know you may want to control your breathing at this time, but relinquish control and let your breath flood your chest cavity.

Imagine that you are in a field of flowers. You're rolling in a meadow and enjoying the soft carpet of greenery. The vivid colors embrace you and cause you to go to your happy place. Do not feel the need to control what time you have to leave from the field. Stay in the field and breathe in and breathe out. Smell the sweet scents floating in the field.

As you are in the field, you may hear background sounds. You may hear the movement of traffic, of cars coming and going. You may also hear the hum of a heating and cooling unit or people moving in the background. Focus on the sound itself briefly, then bring your focus back to your breath. You're connected to those sounds through your breath. You are connected to this Moment by your breathing. Every time you're focused, but get off track, kindly bring it back. While you're focusing on your breath, notice how you may feel the need to have an opinion on this moment.

Maybe you like my voice, maybe you do not, maybe you do not like the position that you're sitting in. Be aware of this tendency to feel like you have to notice what's going on and have an opinion about it. Instead of focusing on the decision to have an opinion, let the need for that go. Throw your opinion away and just be. Focus on the situation as it is. It is not good or bad it is just is. Notice that the only thing that you are focusing on at this time is your breath and the physical sensations that come with your breath cycle.

At this point, you may be feeling slightly uncomfortable, or you're ready to stop. You can deal with the sensations by slowly moving your feet so they do not go to sleep or slightly to appease the discomfort. This may be one way to do with it. Another way to deal with your physical discomfort is to just experience it a little while longer. Allow your discomfort to go one more moment and see what it feels like. Do you feel any tingling or numbness? Embrace it. It will soon pass. You can deal with it, just experience whatever you are feeling right now fully. There is not one better way more than the other.

Notice your intentions at this moment. Remove the intentions and just be. On your next breath, lose your intentions. Focus only on your breath. Breathe in and then breathe out. Notice how everything comes back to your breath. Now if you have gone way off into left field, that's totally okay. Use your breath to bring back attention to your breath.

Embrace the power of your cycle of breathing. Notice how the breath can help you ride the good thoughts and bad thoughts. See that when even you go off to be distracted, you can focus on your breathing and bring it back to just being in the moment without having to make any decision.

Be proud of yourself for noticing that you have gotten off track but you're able to get back into focus with your breath. Great job on being mindful. Keep that thought of mindfulness with you and the importance of breathing as you go along your way.

Now that the meditation is coming to an end, feel proud that you were able to spend this time building your muscle of awareness by breathing. Be grateful that you have been able to spend this time in this present moment and transfer this skill to other moments in your life. Be grateful that you are able to walk day-by-day in the present moment without being judgmental.

Mindfulness Meditation for Relaxation and Stress Relief

Before we begin this meditation, take a few moments to get comfortable and loose. It is now time to turn your mind off from the busy hustle and bustle of everyday grind and just focus on being in the moment. This meditation is to help you be present and relax and relieve any stress that may be penned up.

We will start with a few deep breaths from the depth of your abdomen. Breathe in through your nose and then blow the air out your mouth. Every time you breathe, feel your stomach come as close to your insides as possible and when you breathe out, let out an audible 'aah.' Does your breathing focus on the physical sensations that come with that deep breaths? This time when you inhale open your mouth and breathe through your mouth. Feel the air tickle your teeth on your tongue. Feel your lungs fill with the great life force of air. During this time, put all your troubles to the side. Breathe them out with every exhale that you take.

You no longer need to feel shackled by any pressure you may be feeling. Try to calm your thoughts from racing. Just observe your thoughts as they go by. Do you notice any thoughts that seem to be re-occurring? Do you notice any patterns from the things that you are thinking? Breathe in and let the thoughts go to the side. Breathe in and breathe out.

When you inhale, feel every part of your body that the air touches relaxing. The deeper you inhale, the more you feel relaxed. Every time you exhale, let the tension escape your body.

Start at your feet. Breathe in and stretch the breath upward. When you breathe, feel the breath relaxing your feet and toes.

Feel the air melt in your attention like ice. Breathe in and let your legs, hips, and waist relax. Feel the tension liquify like ice. Next move up to your stomach. Feel the inhale spread the walls of your abdomen. Breathe out and feel the tension in your chest melt away when you exhale. Mentally tell yourself to relax.

Feel your chest filled with air. Feel your entire body dripping with air and feel the warmth in your chest when you exhale. Now, work your way up to your neck. Feel the warmth of the air and warm up your entire neck. Feel the tension leave your neck. You can now breathe in and feel the warmth feel your entire head. Draw I your breath deeply, and then feel yourself relax. Feel your entire body relax as you exhale that breath out.

Be in the moment. Feel calm and be ok with that. Be completely still. Tune out any background noises that you may be hearing. Do not focus on those noises. Focus on your breath. To focus even more, focus on your heartbeat. Notice how it changes with your breath. The deeper your breaths are, the slower your heartbeat is. The faster your breaths are, the faster your heartbeat goes. Keep your breaths, slow and deep.

Do you notice any spots of tension in your body? Breathe in and feel the tension go away with every breath. Bring your head down to your chest and bring it back up. Then push your head back as far as it can go. Stop and enjoy the release. Squeeze your eyes tight and then loosen them. Wrinkle your nose and the area around your bridge. Let the tension go away with every wriggle. Then wiggle your forehead. Then let the tension melt away with every forehead wiggle.

Breathe in and let the tension in your eyes go away again. Shrug your shoulders up. Keep them up and let them go down. Then breathe in and with your breath, let them out slowly. Bring awareness to your arms. Breathe in and then let the arms move upward with your breath and let them go. Move to your wrists and move them back and forth. Stop and then feel the looseness of your wrists.

You should now feel your body in a total state of deep relaxation. Now go back to your thighs. Imagine them being completely relaxed now. Feel your entire body relax. Breathe in and inhale for four counts: 1, 2, 3, 4. Let out your breath before for four counts: 1, 2, 3, 4. The meditation will be coming to an end soon. Slowly open your eyes.

Blink and welcome the day. Now you can stand up and move forward. Keep the feeling of relaxation and stress-free feeling with you as you go about your day-to-day tasks.

Mindfulness Meditation for Inner Peace and Calm

Find a comfortable position by sitting or lying down and close your eyes. This meditation is to help you find inner peace and calm. We will begin by noticing your breath. Please breathe in through your nose and exhale through your mouth.

With every breath, feel the coolness of the air touching every organ with peace as it feels your lungs. Feel your lungs with a breast as deep as you can hold. With every breath, feel the power of your breath and the reinvigoration it brings. With every breath, bring stillness, hope, and peace to your busy mind.

Throughout the meditation, your mind may begin to wonder and focus on different types of things. Gently and firmly guide your thoughts back to your breaths. As you inhale, fuel your body with breath. Feel the breath charging your body and preparing you for whatever comes ahead.

As you exhale, rid itself of any fresh negativity or bad germs that are over your body. With each breath, feel your body being replenished with peace and calm until no more negativity is left. Focus on your breath for 10 counts and then let go.

Breathe in and breathe out. Feel the warmth of your body with every breath. Feel the gentle feeling of lightness that spreads through your body with every single breath that you take.

When you inhale with this breath, repeat, 'I am peaceful.' Think of what brings peace to you. Repeat, 'I am peaceful.'

Exhale and feel negativity being scooped out your body in a pile to the side that you can discard. Do not worry about the negativity. Negativity is the least of your concerns. You are concerned about your breathing and the power of a single breath.

Breathe in and feel relaxed. State to yourself, 'I am calm.' What brings your calmness. Experience a double dose of that calmness by thinking of an image that brings your calm. Think about this image as you continue to inhale and exhale.

With every breath, feel your extremities relax and loosen the tension within until you feel better. Do not feel discouraged if you are not feeling as relaxed as you need to be. Continue to focus on your breathing.

Breathe out slowly and completely. Notice the slight space between every breath cycle. Breathe in and then let your body feel every single ray of relaxation like the sun spreading all over your body.

Breathe in, and repeat, 'I am calm. No matter what.' Do not think of any circumstances that can change your mood, whether those circumstances are good or bad. Focus rather on being calm regardless of the circumstances surrounding you no matter what situation you may find yourself in.

Breathe out and then breathe back in. Feel that you are calm no matter what. Breathe out. Breathe in and feel the breath bringing calmness to you. It anchors you and brings you peace with any situation that you may encounter.

Repeat to yourself, 'I am at peace. No matter what.' Keep this in mind that whatever may be bothering you, feel calm no matter what. Keep the spirit of calmness within you and take it with you as you go.

As we bring this meditation to a close, keep this feeling of peaceful calm centered within you and let it carry you throughout the day. Feel empowered to be present and mindful for a few more moments if you choose to do so. The benefits of mindfulness do not have to be rushed. Take your time and do as you please.

Whenever you are ready, we will end the meditation on the count of five: 1, 2, 3, 4, 5.

Mindfulness meditation for self-compassion
Let's begin by getting in a comfortable and dignified position. You can sit, be in lotus pose, or lie down. Then take in three deep breaths.

Breathe in. Feel the oxygen relax in your entire body. Breathe out. Push the air out as far as you can.

Inhale. Feel like you're sucking in a straw and draw as much as in as possible. Count to four counts: 1, 2, 3, 4. Exhale for four counts: 1, 2, 3, 4. You can let your imaginary straw go.

Inhale one more time. Four counts: 1, 2, 3, 4. Exhale for four counts: 1, 2, 3, 4.

Again, make sure that you are in the most comfortable position possible and switch your focus to the breathing. This meditation is all about being compassionate with yourself. Too many times, we can be our harshest critic. Too many times we can fall victim to trying to comparing ourselves with others. This meditation seeks to disrupt that train of thought. This meditation is all about being compassionate to yourself according to the place that you are at this very moment. Not at the place you were yesterday or will be in the future, but this meditation is all about being grateful for the person that you are at this very moment.

Focus on your breath and be aware of the words that we will be saying. Let the words fill your body space in the same way your breath anchors you. Try and feel the power of your words and the power of your breath at the same time.

If you have any pressing thoughts or any worrisome thoughts that are bothering you like a gnat in the background, swat them away. But if they come back just allow them to be. Make note of those thoughts and bring your attention back to your breath.

Feel where the breath is most obvious to you. Feel it deeply as the breath travels up your nose throughout the rest of your body. When you exhale, feel your breath when it is leaving your body. Feel it taking all of the toxins and negativity of your environment away with it.

Whatever you feel that breath is doing, focus on the sensation of breathing and what your breath cycle looks like. With every inhale, take the nurturing warmth of your breath and let it spread throughout your body just like a pond ripple in your favorite lake.

With every exhale, say, "I am happy." Think of what makes you happy. Think of what delights you. Think of how your body feels when you are in your happy place. Repeat to yourself that "I am happy."

Breathe in and exhale say, "I am safe." Know that you are safe no matter what you may do. Know that you are safe right now as you are mindful. Know that your thoughts are safe. You are in a judgment-free zone. There are no good thoughts or bad thoughts. They are just thoughts.

Breathe in and breathe out. Say, "I am kind to myself." Whatever mistakes you have made in the past, they are gone. Learn from them. Whatever evil, malicious things you have done, they are gone. Say it again, "I am kind to myself." Breathe in and exhale again.

Breathe in and breathe out. Repeat to yourself, "I accept myself for who I am today." Breathe in. And breathe out. You are perfect. Your perfections and imperfections make you the perfect you. Breathe in and breathe out, and say, "I accept myself for who I am today."

Inhale and exhale. Say "I forgive myself." Guess what? Whatever has been done has been done. Forgive yourself from the nice you and mean you. Be gentle, but firm. Learn what you need from every situation. It is there for your reflection and understanding. Breathe in and breathe out. Say, "I forgive myself."

Breathe in. Breathe out, and say, "I am healthy." If you can breathe, you are able to be healthy. If you are breathing, you can always improve your health. Be still in the moment and think of how you can improve your health. If you are already healthy, encourage yourself to stay on the healthy path. Breathe in and breathe out. Say, "I am healthy."

Breathe in. Breathe out. And say, "I practice self-compassion daily." Feel how compassionate you feel for yourself. Know that you are free from judgment. Feel free from harsh judgments of yourself. Feel free from being upset about any mistakes that you have made. Breathe in and breathe out. Repeat again, "I practice self-compassion daily."

Breathe in and breathe out. Feel free to make use of the phrases in whichever order you would like. You can either rest and continue to breathe in and breathe out. Or you can repeat your favorite affirmation.

Whichever you decide, that is fine. There is no right or wrong answer. Do what is most comfortable for you. Whatever you decide, try to be mindful of your decision.

The meditation will be coming to an end soon. Do what you must. If you are enjoying this exercise, and you want to take the time to continue to be mindful, you are able to do that. If you must get up to continue about your day, you can do that as well.

When it's time, slightly awaken your senses and return to the critical mind on the count of three. One. Two. Three.

Open your eyes and be fortified by your self-compassion meditation.

In conclusion, the guided meditations in this chapter can help you get started. They are especially helpful if you are not sure how to begin or what to say if you want to be mindful. These meditations are great to practice the different ways that you can breathe and improve the ways that you can be mindful. Now we will move to a few guided meditations that affect specific sicknesses in the next chapter.

Chapter 5: Healing Mindfulness Meditation Exercises

"If you are facing in the right direction, all you need to do is keep on walking." – Buddha

---

Buddha said it well. Now that you are walking in the right direction of doing your own guided meditations, it is now time for you to keep on walking and learning. The mindfulness meditation exercises in this chapter are going to focus on healing and coping with anxiety, depression, insomnia, and grief. Research has shown that mindfulness meditation is quite beneficial in helping you heal these illnesses due to the boost in mental and heart health. Mindfulness meditation is also a great tool to help with coping with these types of challenges because it also draws on your inner strength and the power of the breath. The following guided mindfulness meditation exercises will help you to relax and cope with the illnesses that you may be dealing with.

Mindfulness Meditation for Anxiety

We will begin our mindfulness meditation for anxiety right now. If you are experiencing anxiety currently or have been experiencing it for a while, I know it is not the best feeling in the world. You may be hurting. You may be scared, but know that you're going to be okay. I know it is hard for you to believe this right now, but know that the responses your body is giving to your anxiety are going to be over soon.

Know that relief from your anxiety is coming. It does not last forever. Do you want to know why? It is because your body has a built-in stress relief already. Your body will naturally deal with anxiety on its own terms. So keep this gem in the back of your mind and know that your body is always helping you deal with your anxiety. It is up to you to activate the stress-relief by being relaxed. It is up to you to help your body relax by taking in deep breaths. The inhales are going to help calm your body. The purpose of this meditation is to use your breathing in order to relax.

You may feel like it is difficult to breathe but be aware that your body is already breathing. Listen to your breath right now. If your breaths are short, try to lengthen your breath by breathing to the count of three. Breathe in for a cycle of three counts; 1, 2, 3. Then breathe out for a breath cycle of three: 1, 2, 3. Notice your heartbeat. Notice if it is going fast or slow.

Let's try to slow your breathing down. Breathe in again. This time we are going to hold the breath cycle for 5 counts. Breathe in: 1, 2, 3, 4, 5. Then breathe out: 1, 2, 3, 4, 5.

Breathe in deeply again. Now breathe out like you're blowing a birthday cake with a lot of candles. You want to make sure that you are blowing each and every one of those candles out. Breathe in and hold your breath in for three counts: 1, 2, 3. Now breathe out slowly: 1, 2, 3. Keep this up. You're doing a great job.

For extra support, you can hold up your fingers and pretend they are the candles in front of you. Now blow the air out open your mouth and make a slight sound as you blow it out. Make a gentle 'hoo' sounds as you let your breath out. You can do this breath cycle one more time, or you can continue to breathe slowly and gently.

Be aware of your body. See how your body is controlling your breathing? Do you see how your body makes sure that your body is getting enough air? Do you see how your body wants to help you calm down? In your comfortable position, close your eyes again and take it all in. Take in how awesome and self-sufficient your body is and how you can help it.

You may still feel overwhelmed. You may feel like no one is with you right now, but know that you are enough. You are your breathing. Your breath is a wave. With every deep inhale you give, the higher the wave is. Ride the wave as high as you can. Breathe in and let your breath out with a big whoosh.

If you want to feel more comfortable, feel free to turn the light off or stand up and pace around as you continue with these breathing exercises. If these steps do not help, know that your anxiety will continue to decrease on its own. You can continue to help your anxiety decrease by breathing. The more you breathe, the calmer you will be. Take it slow. Imagine with that feeling of calm feels like. Is it blue or yellow or white? Is it vivid, pastel, or bold? Feel that the deeper you breathe, the more you relax and the faster your anxiety will go.

As you breathe, feel that they are helping your body relax. With each breath, you breathe in, breathe in deeply and feel your body getting calmer. Please try and focus on your breath right now.

You do not have to worry about what is triggering you or causing you anxiety. You do not have to worry about what you're going to do to deal with the anxiety. The only thing you should focus on is your breathing. Feel the flutter of the clothing against your chest every time you breathe in and breathe out. If you're feeling uncomfortable, and you need to find a more comfortable position do so gently but continue to focus on your breath.

You are going to be okay. I know it doesn't feel like it, but you are going to be okay. Now we want to feel the warmth that's associated with calm. You can warm your hands together gently until you feel your palm slightly warming up. Do not go vigorously - go smoothly, slowly, and gently. Do you feel the warmth?

Now that you can focus on your hands moving, how does it sound? That sound can help you ground yourself from your anxiety and sent to you along with your breathing. When you feel that you focused on your hands enough, you can stop and place your hands by your side and breathe in again.

Relax and know that anxiety is normal. Focus on the sensations of your body. Notice how they're different from when you first began. Listen to the sound your breath makes as you breathe in and you breathe out. Moment by moment, the breath is helping you pass this level of anxiety.

Anxiety is a natural process. It is not always easy to feel, but it is natural. Help your body react by continuing to breathe. Do not have any judgment about your state of mind right now. Know that life happens. But when you're able to be in this moment, just like now, with your breath, you can focus on the good. You can focus on just being. You do not have to make a decision to do anything. Just be here right now with your breath and your body. Know that you're going to be okay.

Accept your body for what it is. Accept your brain for what it gives you. Accept your responses for what they are because they are what they are. affirmations to help you and your body recover. You can either listen and continue to breathe slowly or you can repeat them after with every breath.

Breathe in, and then breathe out. Repeat after me. "I accept who I am no matter what I am feeling." The past does not determine who I am, nor the future. The only thing that matters is the right now and by accepting who you are now, you are being mindful.

Breathe in, and then breathe out. Repeat after me. "I know that anxiety does not last forever. My anxiety will pass." Anxiety feels like it will last forever, but if you take it in the present moment, you will be able to ride the wave to calmness.

Breathe in, and then breathe out. Repeat after me. "My body is prepared to handle my anxiety. I can help by breathing." Be grateful and know that your body can handle any stress that it faces. The most important thing is to help your body out by breathing deeply.

Know that deep down inside, that as each second goes by and as every minute goes by, I feel my anxiety going away. And I feel a large dose of calm replacing it.

Repeat after me. "I feel relaxed. I am more comfortable." As you continue to breathe, notice how the breath is affecting your body.

Breathe in, and then breathe out. Repeat after me. "I accept how I feel right now. I am calm. I'm going to be okay. I am relaxed. I am at peace." Keep breathing. You will continue to feel your body come down from the anxiety that you are experiencing. Pay careful attention to how your body feels in the relaxed state.

Great job. Notice how you feel. Continue to feel relaxed. Continue to breathe in and breathe out. Notice how loose your limbs feel. Notice how easy your breaths come and go. Notice how easy it is for your body to pick up on the next breath after your first one.

Continue to relax for as long as you want. You can continue to stay in your comfortable position and breathe in and breathe out, or you can go ahead and bring the meditation to an end. Whatever you feel like doing, be mindful of the decision.

On the count of three, this meditation will be ending. You can replay this guided meditation again if you need to or continue to breathe deeply and silently on your own. One. Two. Three.

Mindfulness Meditation for Depression

In this meditation, we're going to focus on dealing with depression. Depression can sometimes feel like wearing sopping wet clothes. You want to dry them because you're wearing them, but it is the only pair you have. So you have to

71

wear them wet, which can take a while. If you had a dryer you would put the clothes in there, but you do not, alas you have to let the clothes air-dry. This meditation will help the clothes dry smoother. I want to commend you for taking action for taking the first step of deciding to meditate.

For this meditation, start by being comfortable. You can be in a nice warm place where you won't be disturbed. We will need time for peace and quiet. We're going to start off breathing deeply for my diaphragm and releasing those breaths from our mouth. As we're breathing, switch out the cloud of doom and gloom above you to a cloud of white positive energy right above us. That energy is right over us. Wherever you go, you are able to get energy and positivity from it that can help make you stronger throughout the day. Every time you breathe in, that energy source gets stronger. Every time you breathe out, negativity, fear, anxiety your worries, and your depression gets weaker. The more you breathe, the stronger, your energy source will be.

Now let's imagine that we are at a beautiful lake house. You are in the middle of the forest with beautiful trees around and it smells like pine. The tall trees reach the sky and are tall and shady. You hang under the trees, and it is only you and your cloud of energy. Feel the beautiful, gentle breeze that goes across the lake while you're sending. Breathe in and feel the power level raise up. Feel calm feel at peace.

Now you want to dip your feet into the lake. Do so. You are floating in the middle of the water on a raft. Float on your back and make a ripple in the water with your finger. While you float on your back, you feel that cloud in the warm sunshine giving you energy. You have no room for the depression. It is going smaller. The more you laugh and giggle and enjoy yourself in the water the more it goes away.

While you were at your favorite place on the lake, think of some of your favorite sounds besides the water. What about the laugh of your baby? The giggle of a sibling or relative? The beautiful sound of fresh water dripping on the pine needles. The more you think of beautiful images as you breathe in, the more that cloud gets powered, your depression weakens and the clothes dry. Breathe in and breathe out. With every breath, feel how much dryer your clothes are beginning to feel.

At this time, just enjoy being in this moment. Feel how your body is beginning to relax. You feel so good, warm and relaxed. You could just go to sleep on the water, but you're not going to. Now you're going to stand upon your raft. Feel the sun on you trying out your body, but feel how reinvigorated you are.

Now as you bring yourself back to your body in your critical brain, you're going to breathe in that feeling of peaceful calm and serenity. Carry the feeling with you throughout the day. And then exhale. When you do so, exhale out any negative thoughts and feelings you may have.

Whenever you feel like your body is just soaking wet in soggy clothes, think about this wonderful energy source or your beautiful day at the beach and your lovely energy cloud that can dry you right out. You are able to feel the calmness from your breathing.

With every breath you take, imagine your white, warm ball of energy that is floating above you, replacing your tears with laughs. Imagine that warm cloud of energy replacing every negative thought you have with a positive one. Imagine that warm ball of energy arming you with calmness, strength, and positivity to right any depressive bout you may face.

Imagine the future where depression is no longer an issue for you. What does that day look like where you say goodbye to depression? What will you be wearing? What type of perfume or cologne will you wear? What will be your celebratory dinner? Are you going to celebrate with friends or by yourself?

Breathe in and then breathe out again. Call your awareness to this very moment. Enjoy the quiet calm joy that your breathing brings.

How will your hair look on the day that you beat depression? Are you going to treat yourself to all your favorite things like a massage, shopping spree, or manicure and pedicure? Keep this visualization close. Know that you are capable of using your breath to control your depression.

Breathe in deeply for a 5 count this time: 1, 2, 3, 4, 5. Breathe out and let your breath go out deeply: 1, 2, 3, 4, 5.

On the count of three, we will bring the meditation to a close. If you need to continue to meditate, feel free to do so. We are in no rush to get you to the next activity. Being mindful is all about taking your time to be present and aware of the moment on your own terms. You can go at your own pace. When you are ready, gently open your eyes. One. Two. Three.

Mindfulness Meditation for Insomnia

Before you begin, lie in a comfortable position on a soft surface like your bed, blanket, or couch. Play relaxing music in the background. Once you're comfortable and you're warm begin to concentrate on your breath.

From the deepest part of your stomach, breathe in. Then empty all the air out by opening your mouth and let all the air leave. You do not want a single ounce of air left in your body. Then you want to breathe in again. Repeat this step by slowly filling up your body with as much air as you can. Hold the breath for 3 seconds and then let it out for the count of three as well. Do this breath cycle 4 more times.

Breathe in. And breathe out. Feel like your limbs have just done a very intense workout and you are tired. Your legs and arms are tense and heavy. Your body aches from such an intense workout and you are tired. The only thing you want is to pile into your bed and go to sleep. You want to feel the rejuvenation of sleep to help your aching bones feel better.

Inhale and then exhale. Imagine that you have just had a full cup of warm feeling. Feel how warm your stomach is from the warm liquid as it sloshes in your belly, calming you and bringing you to sleep's shore. The warm, sweet milk makes you feel human and connects you to this month just like your breathing.

Breathe in deeply. Then breathe out just as deeply. Feel that you are in a long car ride taking a long windy road in the middle of nowhere. The road is long and windy, but the scenery is beautiful, and you are in the passenger seat enjoying how long the ride is. Your feet are handing in the dashboard and your window is slightly cracked. You feel the breeze going against your face and you are

Inhale from your diaphragm. Then exhale from just as deep in your diaphragm. Feel how your breath is causing your body to feel groggy and restless. Feel that your body is losing your alertness that you normally have through the day and feel the groggy calm that's overtaking your body.

If you think about any thoughts that interrupting your focus on breathing, gently move them out the way. Now we want to relax your body, so it feels nice and warm and activates your sleep trigger. Imagine you have just eaten a full meal and your stomach is full and plump. You are tired and groggy from a meal of eating all of your favorite foods.

As you breathe, try to feel any tension in your body so your breath can help you release the tension. To begin, we want to start at the head. Squint your eyes as close as possible and then open them until you feel relaxed.

Next, roll your neck from side to side. Put your chin down to your chest and then put your head on the floor. As you do this, feel the tension leave in your body, and in its place feel a nice comfortable, relaxed feeling. Move to your chest breathing as deeply as possible and breathe out. Then focus on your thighs and your legs keep going. You feel a nice warm feeling replacing it.

Next, we're going to feel like all of our anxiety has just disappeared. We're floating on clouds. The clouds wrap you like a blanket and a magic genie. Just keep flying and flowing into your going slowly into sleepland.

Next, we want to feel like we are at your favorite fishing spot or your favorite place in the mountains. The fish are biting at the surface of the lake and in the process making beautiful ripples that keep spreading wider and wider. As you are in the mountains, feel the heat of your body as you are snuggled deeply. You're your snowsuit. When you're in your place, you do not have to worry about going anywhere you are exactly where you need to be.

Breathe in and breathe out. Whatever your thoughts are, let them dissolve away and just focus on your breath. You do not have a set time that you have to be anywhere. There's no pressure to arrive.

Just feel safe and the warmth of being in the clouds. We do not have a care in the world. This is what it feels like. Feel that you are bouncing from cloud to cloud to cloud. You're just floating amongst the airy, pale blue skies. All of the tickles from the cloud are making your tired.

Do one more deep breath and then feel your entire body relax. Feel your arms and legs loosen. Feel your stomach and back gently move back and forth with every soft breath that you take. Feel each breath pushing you to a deep, peaceful sleep.

Keep your eyes closed and feel like a breath in the middle of hibernation. Nothing will be able to wake you up. You are going to rest deeply and peacefully. Just follow your breath until you go to sleep.

Then let the music guide you to the land of slumber.

Mindfulness Meditation for Grief and Loss

This mindfulness meditation is to help you cope with the pain and suffering from grief and loss. Be sure that you are in a comfortable place before we begin. That comfortable place could be sitting in a dignified position in a chair or lying down.

Have a pen and paper handy in case you need to write down anything later. Place your head in a comfortable position, and make sure your body is relaxed. Raise your shoulders up and hold them up before 5 seconds. Then let your shoulders release go and release all the tension out your body. You can also play soft, calming music in the background if you'd like. Take three deep breaths breathing from the very depths of your diaphragm and breathing out through your nose.

Breathe in. Breathe out. Still your thoughts. You are in a judgment-free zone.

Inhale for three counts: 1, 2, 3. And exhale for three counts: 1, 2, 3.

Inhale one more time. Exhale one more time.

Once you feel comfortable, if you feel the painful thoughts come back, that's okay. Do not try to fix the pain. Do not try to deal with the pain. Just feel it.

Breathe in deeply. If you want to cry, feel free to cry. If it feels like you will never ever get over this pain, breathe and brace that feeling filled up with all your pain. You will get over it.

Now take a breath and let the air fully out. Breathe in deeply again. Look at your thoughts neutrally. Now try to look at yourself like you're from the outside looking in. If you could describe yourself, what would it be? What's one good thing that you see about yourself? What's one area of opportunity? What can you learn from this situation?

Where do you feel the most pain? Is it in the middle of your chest or is it in the pit of your stomach? Wherever it is, zone in on your pain. Now that you've located that pain, take in a big breath and feel that the oxygen is healing the pain.

Next, imagine how your loved one will feel. Do you think they will want you to feel this way? If you can hear their voice one more time, what do you think they would say to you? Just listen to their voice and write it down for later. If you do not hear anything, except silence in your breath, that's okay as well.

As you inhale, take in the love that you know you have for the person and exhale then tension out. Feel grounded in this moment and know that things are going to be better. Grief does not last always. The more you breathe in, the more you grow. The more you breathe in, the less grief you have. Ride the wave of breath into calmness.

Know that your loved one is protecting you. Know that they're protecting you. Send love to them and know that the love is reciprocated. You are one in spirit and in mind. They are guiding you and sending rays of warmth, love and positive energy to you so that you know that you are not alone.

Feel the relaxation coming over you. Do not run away from the emotion. Now instead of feeling like the sadness, focus on the good times. The fun, the laughter, the realness. Take more deep breaths and bring energy into your body. Know that you're never alone. Replenish your broken heart with breaths and with positive affirmations.

Breathe in and then breathe out. Repeat after me, "I am loved." You are loved by yourself, and you are loved by your loved one. The pain you are feeling shows that someone loved you and you loved someone too.

Breathe in and then breathe out. Repeat after me. "I had precious valuable time with my loved one, and I know that I will get through this." The old cliché is true: 'Time heals all wounds.'

Breathe in and then breathe out. Repeat after me. "I know that grief and pain will not last forever." Just like anxiety, just like pain from hitting your big toe on the side of the bed, pain is temporary and one day you will not even feel the pain.

Breathe in and then breathe out. Repeat after me. "I know that the lessons and time I spend with the loved one will help me make it." Think about the words that you learned from your loved one. Let those words comfort you like your favorite blanket.

Breathe in and then breathe out. Repeat after me: "I am wiser, stronger, and I am ready for whatever lies ahead." You are strong, brave, kind and tough. You will get through this.

Breathe in and then breathe out. Hold the in-between space between your next breath. Now breathe in and breath out one more time.

On three, gently open your eyes and awaken. Keep the feelings of love, calmness, and feelings of happiness with you throughout the day.

In conclusion, this chapter continued to build on the previous chapter by giving you guided meditation scripts to use that target specific issues that you may be experiencing like stress, depression, grief, or insomnia. Each scripted meditation uses a combination of breathing, relaxation and visualization techniques to guide you through each session. Feel free to use them as is or modify each meditation as you see fit. You can use each one as a basis to build your own meditations as well. Remember, every time you meditate you improves, so please continue to practice.

Conclusion

"Be where you are, otherwise you will miss your life." – Buddha

Thank you for making it through to the end of Mindfulness Meditation: A Practical Guide for Beginners, let's hope it was informative and able to provide you with all of the tools you need to achieve your goals whatever they may be. If you can only take one thing away from this book, please take this, please know that mindfulness can transform your life. If can be the difference between a regular life or a life that's appreciated and full of gratitude. If you are on the track to being more mindful in your everyday life, know that you are on a journey that will unleash wonderful surprises in your life.

The next step is to find your special place so you can begin your mindful meditation practice. You can even go ahead and create your list of affirmations that you can use throughout your sessions. You can revisit any of your special phrases in the book that you marked to check out at any other time. Feel free to join any support group that can help answer any questions you may have along the way. There are great resources to check out online. You can also check out location meditation groups on Craigslist or find a Meetup site. Also, try to eat healthily and sleep well. The better you take care of your body, the better your meditation session will be. Overall health also helps you to be more mindful in your day-to-day life.

Remember, that you do not have to do everything right the right time when you meditate. As you progress in your practice, you will continue to improve. Embrace the journey. Lastly, do not stop learning. This book about: *Mindfulness and Meditation* is a great foundation to have, but continue to build on it. Continue to learn more about how the benefits of mindfulness meditation affect you. You can also continue to work on meditation by using guided meditations until you are at the point where you can do the meditations on your own without the help of guided meditations. This journey is to last a lifetime and the more prepared you are the more you will be prepared to sustain and improve your mindfulness meditation practice along the way.

Lastly, if you enjoyed this book I ask that you please take the time to review it on Audible.com. Your honest feedback would be greatly appreciated.

Thank you.

Now, I would like to share with you a free sneak peek to another one of my books that I think you will really enjoy. The book is called "Self Compassion: The Mindful Path to Understand your Emotions" by Kirstin Germer, Christopher Neff and it's A Practical Guide to Learn the Proven Power of Self-Acceptance, Self-Criticism, Self-Awareness and Mindfulness. You will also learn how to be Kind to Yourself and Move On.

Enjoy!

Introduction

Fostering a sense of self-compassion and self-acceptance can be challenging even for a healthy and well-rounded adult. Despite how important these two characteristics are, very few people are taught about how to utilize them in their personal lives. Instead, we are often taught to be hard on ourselves, push ourselves as far as we can, and demand the maximum results out of our efforts. While challenging yourself to achieve substantial growth is valuable, pushing yourself to the point where it becomes self-sabotaging is not a positive habit to support.

If you truly want to achieve all of the success that you desire in life, you need to have a clear understanding of your mental wellbeing and around how you can support it so that you can improve your chances of succeeding. Without a strong mindset to back them up, most people will fail to achieve their desired level of success because despite having the best of intentions, they will struggle to keep themselves focused and motivated. Through the emotional and mental self-sabotaging behaviors such as having an overly harsh inner critic or trying to push through challenging emotions without acknowledging their purpose or healing them, they will simply burn out and fail to thrive.

As you listen through this book, realize that you are going to be granted every single tool you need to begin developing the skills to become more self-compassionate and self-accepting. From identifying how to feel your emotions and develop a relationship to building a productive mindfulness and self-awareness practice, everything is devoted to helping you motivate yourself in a healthy way. The tools in this book will not encourage or motivate you to become complacent, lose focus, or stop aiming for your dreams with any less intensity than you already have been. Instead, they will support you in having a stronger focus on how you can achieve your goals without compromising your inner sense of wellbeing. As a result, all of the success that you earn in your life will feel far more meaningful and positive.

If self-compassion has been particularly challenging for you until now, or if the concept itself seems foreign, I encourage you to really set the intention to approach this book and the subjects within it with an open mind. You will get the most out of each chapter and all of the tools provided if you give yourself permission to see things from a new perspective at least for the duration of this book. Fully embrace the practice of not only learning about and understanding these concepts and tools but actually working towards putting them into practice in your life as well. As you begin to see just how powerful they are and how they support you in moving forward towards a more positive future, you will quickly begin to realize why they matter so much.

Lastly, there is one major concept that you need to realize before you begin listening this book. That is — self-compassion is an act of self-care, but it is also a tool that is learned through personal development practices. You are not going to be able to achieve self-compassion all in one attempt, nor will you truly be able to measure or grade yourself on the level of self-compassion that you currently have or that you develop. While there are ways for you to track your improvements and we will go into detail on those ways later, you need to understand that this practice is solely about helping yourself feel better and feel more positive in your approach to life. By allowing yourself to embody that balance, you will begin to feel far more peaceful overall.

Now, if you are ready to embark on the next chapter of your journey in self-development, it is time that you begin! Remember, self-compassion is a powerful tool for you to equip yourself with, so approach this book as open-mindedly as you possibly can. And of course, enjoy the process!

Chapter 1: Understanding the Self

Your Self or your identity is an important element of who you are. When you consider who you are, the illusion that you come up with is how you identify yourself. Although we tend to believe that our selves are an inherent part of who we are and that our personal beliefs over ourselves are finite and final, the reality is that who we are and who we think we are, typically reflect two entirely different people. Many people fail to realize that there is a difference and often find themselves genuinely believing that they are the person whom they envision in their minds and that there is no other alternative or option. As a result, they may end up developing a highly toxic, unrealistic, and self-sabotaging image or belief around who they are.

Realizing that who you truly are and who you think you are is two different people can come as a sense of relief to many. When you discover that there is a good chance that you do not actually align with the images or beliefs you have created, you realize that there is an opportunity for you to see yourself in a new light. You may even get the opportunity to start seeing yourself more clearly for who you really are, rather than for the illusion that you have been holding onto in your mind. In fact, by detaching from the strict identity you have held onto in your mind, you can give yourself the opportunity to begin experiencing far more compassion towards yourself in your life.

Identity is a rather complex topic that extends far beyond the image we carry of ourselves and the image that other's carry. In fact, there is an entire psychological study devoted to understanding identity and your sense of self and helping you discover exactly "who" you are. This field of study is known as social science and is comprised of psychologists and researchers who are actively seeking to understand identity to an even deeper level and get a clear sense of what makes a person's identity. Because there are so many different levels of identity, the study itself is quite expansive and continues to discover what one's true identity is versus the way they identify themselves and the way others identify them. In the following sections, you are going to get a deeper insight into what your sense of self truly is, how it is made up, and how your sense of self impacts the way you live your life.

Discovering the Multiple Selves

There are two ways that people have multiple sense of self. The first way that you can experience multiple senses of self comes from how you interact with the people around you and the identity you possess around these people. For example, the self you are around your friends is likely quite different from the self you are around your family or your co-workers. Your environment is a huge factor in which role you will play, depending on where you are and who you are actively surrounded by. The second way that you experience multiple social selves is determined between the way you perceive yourself and the way others perceive you. Since everyone has had their own unique interactions and experiences with you, it is not unreasonable to realize that everyone sees you slightly different from how others see you. For example, your best friend may see you completely different from how your other friends may see you, or your Grandma may carry a completely different belief of who you are compared to the rest of the world. The relationship that people share with you, the experiences that you share together, and their perception of you and of people in general will all impact how people identify you. As a result, you actually have multiple identities – and no, that does not mean that you are having an identity crisis or that you have something wrong with you. It is actually entirely normal to have many identities.

When it comes to identifying yourself, you must realize that on a psychological front, you are not identifying yourself as one person inhabiting one body. You are identifying yourself based on the actual identity that you carry or the characteristics and personality traits that you are perceived to have. Your "self" is the conscious aspect of you that interacts with the world around you, communicates with other people, and shares experiences with others. Although there is no scientific evidence that proves that there is an out-of-body "self," most psychologists believe that the self is not attached to or identified by a person's body. Instead, it is the dimension of you that exists in your mind or the aspects of you that make up "who" you are beyond your physical and biological self.

This part of yourself that is not defined by your body or biology is typically described in three related but separable domains when it comes to psychological understanding. This means that there are three elements that coincide to make up your "self" or your identity. The first domain is known as your experiential self which is also known as the 'theatre of consciousness.' This part of yourself is identified as your first-person sense of being or how you personally experience the world around you. This part of yourself remains consistent over periods of time which results in psychologists believing that it is very closely linked to your memory. The second part of your identity is what is known as your private self-consciousness. This is your inner narrator or the voice that verbally narrates what is happening in your life to you privately within your mind. When you are reading, learning, or interpreting the world around you, this voice is actively narrating how you are interpreting that information and what sense you are making of it. This is the part of you that carries your beliefs and values about how the world works. Neuroscientist Antonio Damasio calls your private self-consciousness your autobiographical self because it is regularly narrating your autobiography in your mind. The third and final dimension of your identity is your public self or your persona. This is the image that you attempt to project to others through your actions, attitudes, behaviors, and words. This is the part of your self that other people interact with and see which results in this being the part of yourself that people generate perceptions around. It is through your persona that people determine what your identity is according to them and their own understanding.

With all that being said, the multiple selves that you embody comes from the persona that you share with others. People will then generate perceptions around who you are, what your identity is, and how they feel about that. It is through this persona that people will decide if they can relate to you, if they like you, and anything else relating to how they feel about you. In realizing that people generate their perceptions of you based off of one single aspect of who you truly are, it helps you realize that their perspective is not accurate. In fact, neither is yours. No one, including yourself, *truly* knows who you actually are. Everything is just generated based on beliefs, values, perspectives, and understandings that have been accumulated through varying life experiences.

Relationship with Ourselves

The relationship that you share with yourself often develops somewhere between the first and second dimensions of your identity. The way you interpret and interact with the world around you, combined with your beliefs and values helps you generate a sort of self-awareness that allows you to begin determining what you believe your identity is. Again, just like with other people, your identity is largely based off of your perception and understanding of the world around you and how it works. Even if your own perception is rarely accurate when compared to who you actually are which is a unique blend of all three layers of your dimensional identity.

Because your relationship with yourself is largely defined by your beliefs and values and your ability to live in alignment with them or not, it is easy to realize that how you identify yourself can be easily shifted based on your perceptions. If you carry certain core beliefs about how people should live, for example, and you are not living in alignment with those beliefs, then you may generate a perception that identifies you as someone who is bad or unworthy. You might relate yourself to the identities you have mentally designed for other people in society who you believe to be bad too which can result in you seeing yourself in an extremely negative light. If you carry certain core beliefs about how people should live and you *are* living in alignment with them, you may praise yourself and see yourself as good and special. You might then find yourself relating more to people in society who you see as good and positive, thus allowing you to cast yourself in a positive light.

The reality is that none of us are truly inherently good or bad, we are all just perceiving, experiencing, and responding to the world around us. Generating internal images of what is positive and what is not only results in you setting standards for yourself on how you should behave. If these standards are beyond what you can reasonably achieve or do not align with what you genuinely want in life, then you may find yourself adhering to beliefs and values that are actually rather destructive. Instead of helping you live a life of contentment and satisfaction, you may find these beliefs leading to you constantly feeling incapable and under confident. As a result, your relationship with yourself may deteriorate because the way in which you view yourself is not reasonable or compassionate.

Everyone Has Their Own Filters and Explanatory Styles

To help you develop your understanding of how your perception of yourself varies from other's perception of you, let's discuss personal filters and explanatory styles. Understanding why everyone has such different views of the world allows you to have a stronger understanding as to why there are so many aspects of your identity based on your own personas and the way that people perceive them and you. The concept of personal filters and explanatory styles is simple. A personal filter is how you see the world and your explanatory style is how you explain it to yourself and to others.

Every single person has a unique filter and explanatory style that is based on their own unique experiences in life. All of the interactions they have had, the situations they have encountered, and things they have been told by the people around them shape the way that they view life itself. How each of these small yet impactful things come together will shape how each person perceives the world around them, others that cohabit the planet with them, and themselves. So, for example, if someone along the way has learned that not washing your dishes every day is a sign of laziness and ignorance, then that person is going to believe that anyone who leaves dishes in the sink overnight is somehow "bad," including themselves.

The foundation of a person's filters and explanatory styles are rooted in childhood when a child is not yet able to generate their own independent thoughts and beliefs. Until we are six years old, our ability to critically think about things and generate our own opinions independent of the opinions of others is virtually non-existent so we absorb everything we learn. This means that anything your parents said, people around you were saying, or you were shown through other's behaviors and actions were anchored into your mind as the foundation of your personal beliefs and values. Even though you gained the capacity to think critically and start generating your own opinions around six years old, you were still actively internalizing what everyone told you because, in most cases, no one ever taught you otherwise. As a result, you likely have many different beliefs and values that stemmed in your childhood which have gone on to impact you for years to come. In fact, these very beliefs and values are believed to make up a lot of what your autobiographical-self narrates to yourself on a daily basis, thus shaping the way you see yourself. See, who you think you are may not even be an accurate reflection of how *you* think, it may actually be an internalization based on the beliefs and values you were taught by people as you were growing up.

Since every single person will hear different things throughout their lives even if they are raised in similar environments, the way that every person views and interprets the world around them varies. Even siblings will grow up to have different perceptions and beliefs based on the way that they have internalized the beliefs they heard and were shown throughout their lifetimes. It is through this process that each person develops their own personal filters and explanatory styles for how they interpret and explain the world around them. Because of this, we can conclude that any beliefs that you have around who you are and any beliefs that others have around who you are do not actually define who you truly are. Instead, they define the belief systems that you have established throughout your life until this point.

When you realize that your beliefs are what shape your *perception* of your identity and not your identity itself, it becomes a lot easier for you to have compassion for yourself. You begin to realize that how you see yourself is not necessarily a true reflection of who you are, but instead a way that you have been lead to view yourself. This view was designed to support you in feeling connected to your 'tribe' or family and community, but in some cases, it can become destructive and result in you feeling deeply disconnected from yourself. When that happens, realizing that you are not inherently 'bad' or 'wrong' because you do not feel like you fit in makes it a lot easier for you to have compassion for your feelings and for the experiences you are going through. As a result, healing from these painful emotions and moving forward into a more self-compassionate and self-loving future becomes a lot easier for you.

Thank you, this preview in now finished.

If you enjoyed this preview of my book "Self Compassion: The Mindful Path to Understand your Emotions" by Kirstin Germer and Christopher Neff, be sure to check out the full book on Amazon.com

Thank you.

The Mindful Path to Self-Compassion

Discover How to Positively Embrace Your Negative Emotions with Self-Awareness and Self-Acceptance, Even if You're Constantly Too Hard on Yourself

Congratulations on purchasing Self Compassion: The Mindful Path to Understand your Emotions, and thank you for doing so!

Every effort was made to ensure it is full of as much useful information as possible. Please enjoy!

Table of Contents

Introduction

Fostering a sense of self-compassion and self-acceptance can be challenging even for a healthy and well-rounded adult. Despite how important these two characteristics are, very few people are taught about how to utilize them in their personal lives. Instead, we are often taught to be hard on ourselves, push ourselves as far as we can, and demand the maximum results out of our efforts. While challenging yourself to achieve substantial growth is valuable, pushing yourself to the point where it becomes self-sabotaging is not a positive habit to support.

If you truly want to achieve all of the success that you desire in life, you need to have a clear understanding of your mental wellbeing and around how you can support it so that you can improve your chances of succeeding. Without a strong mindset to back them up, most people will fail to achieve their desired level of success because despite having the best of intentions, they will struggle to keep themselves focused and motivated. Through the emotional and mental self-sabotaging behaviors such as having an overly harsh inner critic or trying to push through challenging emotions without acknowledging their purpose or healing them, they will simply burn out and fail to thrive.

As you listen through this book, realize that you are going to be granted every single tool you need to begin developing the skills to become more self-compassionate and self-accepting. From identifying how to feel your emotions and develop a relationship to building a productive mindfulness and self-awareness practice, everything is devoted to helping you motivate yourself in a healthy way. The tools in this book will not encourage or motivate you to become complacent, lose focus, or stop aiming for your dreams with any less intensity than you already have been. Instead, they will support you in having a stronger focus on how you can achieve your goals without compromising your inner sense of wellbeing. As a result, all of the success that you earn in your life will feel far more meaningful and positive.

If self-compassion has been particularly challenging for you until now, or if the concept itself seems foreign, I encourage you to really set the intention to approach this book and the subjects within it with an open mind. You will get the most out of each chapter and all of the tools provided if you give yourself permission to see things from a new perspective at least for the duration of this book. Fully embrace the practice of not only learning about and understanding these concepts and tools but actually working towards putting them into practice in your life as well. As you begin to see just how powerful they are and how they support you in moving forward towards a more positive future, you will quickly begin to realize why they matter so much.

Lastly, there is one major concept that you need to realize before you begin to read this book. That is — self-compassion is an act of self-care, but it is also a tool that is learned through personal development practices. You are not going to be able to achieve self-compassion all in one attempt, nor will you truly be able to measure or grade yourself on the level of self-compassion that you currently have or that you develop. While there are ways for you to track your improvements and we will go into detail on those ways later, you need to understand that this practice is solely about helping yourself feel better and feel more positive in your approach to life. By allowing yourself to embody that balance, you will begin to feel far more peaceful overall.

Now, if you are ready to embark on the next chapter of your journey in self-development, it is time that you begin! Remember, self-compassion is a powerful tool for you to equip yourself with, so approach this book as open-mindedly as you possibly can. And of course, enjoy the process!

Chapter 1: Understanding the Self

Your Self or your identity is an important element of who you are. When you consider who you are, the illusion that you come up with is how you identify yourself. Although we tend to believe that our selves are an inherent part of who we are and that our personal beliefs over ourselves are finite and final, the reality is that who we are and who we think we are, typically reflect two entirely different people. Many people fail to realize that there is a difference and often find themselves genuinely believing that they are the person whom they envision in their minds and that there is no other alternative or option. As a result, they may end up developing a highly toxic, unrealistic, and self-sabotaging image or belief around who they are.

Realizing that who you truly are and who you think you are is two different people can come as a sense of relief to many. When you discover that there is a good chance that you do not actually align with the images or beliefs you have created, you realize that there is an opportunity for you to see yourself in a new light. You may even get the opportunity to start seeing yourself more clearly for who you really are, rather than for the illusion that you have been holding onto in your mind. In fact, by detaching from the strict identity you have held onto in your mind, you can give yourself the opportunity to begin experiencing far more compassion towards yourself in your life.

Identity is a rather complex topic that extends far beyond the image we carry of ourselves and the image that other's carry. In fact, there is an entire psychological study devoted to understanding identity and your sense of self and helping you discover exactly "who" you are. This field of study is known as social science and is comprised of psychologists and researchers who are actively seeking to understand identity to an even deeper level and get a clear sense of what makes a person's identity. Because there are so many different levels of identity, the study itself is quite expansive and continues to discover what one's true identity is versus the way they identify themselves and the way others identify them. In the following sections, you are going to get a deeper insight into what your sense of self truly is, how it is made up, and how your sense of self impacts the way you live your life.

Discovering the Multiple Selves

There are two ways that people have multiple sense of self. The first way that you can experience multiple senses of self comes from how you interact with the people around you and the identity you possess around these people. For example, the self you are around your friends is likely quite different from the self you are around your family or your co-workers. Your environment is a huge factor in which role you will play, depending on where you are and who you are actively surrounded by. The second way that you experience multiple social selves is determined between the way you perceive yourself and the way others perceive you. Since everyone has had their own unique interactions and experiences with you, it is not unreasonable to realize that everyone sees you slightly different from how others see you. For example, your best friend may see you completely different from how your other friends may see you, or your Grandma may carry a completely different belief of who you are compared to the rest of the world. The relationship that people share with you, the experiences that you share together, and their perception of you and of people in general will all impact how people identify you. As a result, you actually have multiple identities – and no, that does not mean that you are having an identity crisis or that you have something wrong with you. It is actually entirely normal to have many identities.

When it comes to identifying yourself, you must realize that on a psychological front, you are not identifying yourself as one person inhabiting one body. You are identifying yourself based on the actual identity that you carry or the characteristics and personality traits that you are perceived to have. Your "self" is the conscious aspect of you that interacts with the world around you, communicates with other people, and shares experiences with others. Although there is no scientific evidence that proves that there is an out-of-body "self," most psychologists believe that the self is not attached to or identified by a person's body. Instead, it is the dimension of you that exists in your mind or the aspects of you that make up "who" you are beyond your physical and biological self.

This part of yourself that is not defined by your body or biology is typically described in three related but separable domains when it comes to psychological understanding. This means that there are three elements that coincide to make up your "self" or your identity. The first domain is known as your experiential self which is also known as the 'theatre of consciousness.' This part of yourself is identified as your first-person sense of being or how you personally experience the world around you. This part of yourself remains consistent over periods of time which results in psychologists believing that it is very closely linked to your memory. The second part of your identity is what is known as your private self-consciousness. This is your inner narrator or the voice that verbally narrates what is happening in your life to you privately within your mind. When you are reading, learning, or interpreting the world around you, this voice is actively narrating how you are interpreting that information and what sense you are making of it. This is the part of you that carries your beliefs and values about how the world works. Neuroscientist Antonio Damasio calls your private self-consciousness your autobiographical self because it is regularly narrating your autobiography in your mind. The third and final dimension of your identity is your public self or your persona. This is the image that you attempt to project to others through your actions, attitudes, behaviors, and words. This is the part of your self that other people interact with and see which results in this being the part of yourself that people generate perceptions around. It is through your persona that people determine what your identity is according to them and their own understanding.

With all that being said, the multiple selves that you embody comes from the persona that you share with others. People will then generate perceptions around who you are, what your identity is, and how they feel about that. It is through this persona that people will decide if they can relate to you, if they like you, and anything else relating to how they feel about you. In realizing that people generate their perceptions of you based off of one single aspect of who you truly are, it helps you realize that their perspective is not accurate. In fact, neither is yours. No one, including yourself, *truly* knows who you actually are. Everything is just generated based on beliefs, values, perspectives, and understandings that have been accumulated through varying life experiences.

Relationship with Ourselves

The relationship that you share with yourself often develops somewhere between the first and second dimensions of your identity. The way you interpret and interact with the world around you, combined with your beliefs and values helps you generate a sort of self-awareness that allows you to begin determining what you believe your identity is. Again, just like with other people, your identity is largely based off of your perception and understanding of the world around you and how it works. Even if your own perception is rarely accurate when compared to who you actually are which is a unique blend of all three layers of your dimensional identity.

Because your relationship with yourself is largely defined by your beliefs and values and your ability to live in alignment with them or not, it is easy to realize that how you identify yourself can be easily shifted based on your perceptions. If you carry certain core beliefs about how people should live, for example, and you are not living in alignment with those beliefs, then you may generate a perception that identifies you as someone who is bad or unworthy. You might relate yourself to the identities you have mentally designed for other people in society who you believe to be bad too which can result in you seeing yourself in an extremely negative light. If you carry certain core beliefs about how people should live and you *are* living in alignment with them, you may praise yourself and see yourself as good and special. You might then find yourself relating more to people in society who you see as good and positive, thus allowing you to cast yourself in a positive light.

The reality is that none of us are truly inherently good or bad, we are all just perceiving, experiencing, and responding to the world around us. Generating internal images of what is positive and what is not only results in you setting standards for yourself on how you should behave. If these standards are beyond what you can reasonably achieve or do not align with what you genuinely want in life, then you may find yourself adhering to beliefs and values that are actually rather destructive. Instead of helping you live a life of contentment and satisfaction, you may find these beliefs leading to you constantly feeling incapable and under confident. As a result, your relationship with yourself may deteriorate because the way in which you view yourself is not reasonable or compassionate.

Everyone Has Their Own Filters and Explanatory Styles

To help you develop your understanding of how your perception of yourself varies from other's perception of you, let's discuss personal filters and explanatory styles. Understanding why everyone has such different views of the world allows you to have a stronger understanding as to why there are so many aspects of your identity based on your own personas and the way that people perceive them and you. The concept of personal filters and explanatory styles is simple. A personal filter is how you see the world and your explanatory style is how you explain it to yourself and to others.

Every single person has a unique filter and explanatory style that is based on their own unique experiences in life. All of the interactions they have had, the situations they have encountered, and things they have been told by the people around them shape the way that they view life itself. How each of these small yet impactful things come together will shape how each person perceives the world around them, others that cohabit the planet with them, and themselves. So, for example, if someone along the way has learned that not washing your dishes every day is a sign of laziness and ignorance, then that person is going to believe that anyone who leaves dishes in the sink overnight is somehow "bad," including themselves.

The foundation of a person's filters and explanatory styles are rooted in childhood when a child is not yet able to generate their own independent thoughts and beliefs. Until we are six years old, our ability to critically think about things and generate our own opinions independent of the opinions of others is virtually non-existent so we absorb everything we learn. This means that anything your parents said, people around you were saying, or you were shown through other's behaviors and actions were anchored into your mind as the foundation of your personal beliefs and values. Even though you gained the capacity to think critically and start generating your own opinions around six years old, you were still actively internalizing what everyone told you because, in most cases, no one ever taught you otherwise. As a result, you likely have many different beliefs and values that stemmed in your childhood which have gone on to impact you for years to come. In fact, these very beliefs and values are believed to make up a lot of what your autobiographical-self narrates to yourself on a daily basis, thus shaping the way you see yourself. See, who you think you are may not even be an accurate reflection of how *you* think, it may actually be an internalization based on the beliefs and values you were taught by people as you were growing up.

Since every single person will hear different things throughout their lives even if they are raised in similar environments, the way that every person views and interprets the world around them varies. Even siblings will grow up to have different perceptions and beliefs based on the way that they have internalized the beliefs they heard and were shown throughout their lifetimes. It is through this process that each person develops their own personal filters and explanatory styles for how they interpret and explain the world around them. Because of this, we can conclude that any beliefs that you have around who you are and any beliefs that others have around who you are do not actually define who you truly are. Instead, they define the belief systems that you have established throughout your life until this point.

When you realize that your beliefs are what shape your *perception* of your identity and not your identity itself, it becomes a lot easier for you to have compassion for yourself. You begin to realize that how you see yourself is not necessarily a true reflection of who you are, but instead a way that you have been lead to view yourself. This view was designed to support you in feeling connected to your 'tribe' or family and community, but in some cases, it can become destructive and result in you feeling deeply disconnected from yourself. When that happens, realizing that you are not inherently 'bad' or 'wrong' because you do not feel like you fit in makes it a lot easier for you to have compassion for your feelings and for the experiences you are going through. As a result, healing from these painful emotions and moving forward into a more self-compassionate and self-loving future becomes a lot easier for you.

Your Environment and Your Values

We have already discussed the nature of values but you may be wondering where *exactly* your values come from and why you develop them in the first place. In "The Four Agreements" by author Don Miguel Ruiz describes humans as being self-domesticated creatures. His take on it is that we learned how to organize ourselves into societies and develop basic rules and regulations for those societies. These rules are designed to keep us safe and help us all work together to contribute to the greater good of society without the vicious outbursts of quarreling or fighting to the death like we often see happening in other species. In order for us to adhere to these rules and continue working together as a society and not be punished by society for breaking those rules, we develop values. These values help us determine what is right and what is wrong so that we can navigate domesticated living and continue being accepted by and welcomed into our society. When we act 'right', we are appreciated, loved, and nurtured. When we act 'wrong', we are punished, shunned, and outcast by our loved ones or our community.

Rules and values are generally a very positive thing that helps us to maintain a positive society that continues to operate effectively and productively. When it comes to looking at our communities as a whole, these support us in determining how we can all cohabit our cities, provinces or states, countries, and continents in a way that is consistent and agreed upon. Although not every locality is governed in the same way, the way that each locality is governed is agreed upon and is accepted by other governed localities. That way, everyone is able to coexist without having to experience the worry of being harmed by anyone else in the community and if it does happen, the person who committed the harming will be penalized for their actions.

Of course, society has its flaws and not everyone is held accountable for their actions, but the general structure works towards keeping everyone together and keeping our societies 'civilized' and functional. Unfortunately, the structure ends up falling down into cliques or areas of society where the specific values and beliefs are more strict and specific than the general society. In a standard society, the values and rules are generally simple. Typically, they involve things like do not harm others and obey the laws so that everyone cooperates in a uniformed way that minimizes the harms to others and keeps the society functioning and moving forward. In subsections of society such as within different cultures, religions, neighborhoods, or even within families and social circles, different values often arise.

Typically, these values are a lot more specific and restrictive than the overall values of any given society. These also tend to be the values that we adopt throughout our lifetimes and are the foundation upon which we decide everything including right from wrong. Through these more restrictive values, we are typically lead to walk a very specific path in order to keep us being accepted and loved by our social circles. We learn these values through our parents' parenting styles, the words of our friends, and the harsh words of bullies. As we listen to the people close to us communicate, gossip, and either praise or reprimand each other for their behaviors, we develop an inner system of values. These values are meant to help us fit in, not only with society as a whole but with our subsection of society within which we were raised. This is how we are able to stay close and connected with the people that we care about and accepted into our personal 'tribes.'

Where our environment can begin to become toxic is when it supports us in developing values that do not actually match our personal beliefs and opinions. For example, say you are raised in a community that believes in Christian and Christian teachings, but you personally feel a deeper connection with Buddhism and Buddhist teachings. In this scenario, the values that you have learned throughout your life may prevent you from pursuing your desired life path because you fear that you will be shunned or punished by your loved ones. Although you would not be reprimanded by society as a whole, you would likely experience friction with the people you are closest with which could make it feel as though you are being completely abandoned or separated from your 'herd' or group. The fear of being separated results in you feeling the same sensations that a wild animal may feel if they were separated from their own herd — anxious, fearful, stressed out and worried about their ability to survive. Of course, choosing to go your own way in a civilized society will likely not result in overly negative or life-threatening repercussions but it is definitely a stressful experience.

The very fear of being shunned leads many people to find themselves accepting and living by values that are not their own so that they can avoid having to be isolated from their group. As they continue to adhere to the values they do not personally believe in, the person will continue to generate feelings of 'I am bad' or 'I am wrong.' These feelings will continue to grow as long as the values a person is accepting and living by are not in alignment with the beliefs that they genuinely have inside. You may understand exactly what this feels like if you are currently living in a state where the values that you are attempting to live by do not accurately reflect how you feel about life itself.

Discover and Understand Your Emotions

Although values can be powerful in helping societies grow together and stay functional, they can also lead to deep inner struggles with varying thoughts and challenging emotions. This is especially true for people living in an environment that does not accurately reflect their personal values and beliefs. The more you live out of alignment with your personal values, the more your autobiographical voice will become plagued with negative thoughts that bully you. The words you have heard from your own bullies or as others were gossiping about people who were not deemed "acceptable" by your group will ring through your mind. Each time you behave or think in a way that you know would be considered bad or wrong by your group, you will play out thoughts in your mind such as 'Why can't I just be normal?' 'Why am I so bad at everything?' or 'Why can I never get it right?' As these thoughts continue playing out, you will find yourself feeling a deteriorating sense of self-esteem and self-confidence. Your ability to feel worthy and capable will diminish as you continually hold yourself up to standards that do not accurately reflect what you value or believe.

In order to step out of the traps of these negative values and belief systems, you have to begin exploring the emotions that are keeping you trapped. You need to begin paying attention to how you are feeling, what your different thoughts are bringing up for you, and how your emotions are impacting your life. By assessing your overall emotional state and getting really clear on what you are actually feeling inside, you can begin to discover whether or not you are actively living in alignment with your *true* values. If you are not, you will need to begin making changes so that you can start living a life that feels more aligned for you, which we will get deeper into later on.

In the meantime, recognizing your ongoing emotional state will give you a general idea as to whether or not your current sense of self is accurate and productive or inaccurate and destructive. If you are living in a chronic state of emotional turmoil and consistently feeling overwhelmed, worthless, unmotivated, or plagued by low self-esteem and low self-confidence, you can pretty much guarantee that your perception of your identity is flawed. It is likely that you are presently struggling to meet your personal values so your autobiographical self continues to attempt to help you 'fit in' to an identity that you do not actually fit into. As a result, each time you act out of alignment with that identity, your autobiographical self reprimands you the same way that people in your group or society would reprimand you if they knew what you were doing or thinking. Although the function of this aspect of yourself is designed to help you fit in and stay protected, it can also become highly damaging and create intense feelings of self-loathing and unworthiness. For that reason, it is important that you identify if and when it is acting out of your best interest so that you can take back control and begin acting in deeper alignment with who you *really* are.

If your emotions are generally positive or content but you find yourself occasionally feeling intense bursts of emotional turmoil, chances are you are living in alignment with your core values for the most part. However, there are likely specific times in your life where your personal values and the external values (or the values of those around you) are not in alignment. As a result, you may find yourself feeling angry, sad, or fearful because you worry that if you do not meet the values of the other person, you will not be 'accepted.' In this case, you may not need to make as drastic of changes, but you will still need to take control over your mind, your inner beliefs, and your chosen behaviors to ensure that you are staying true to your inner self.

The best way to discover and understand your emotions is to begin journaling on a regular basis. Writing down your thoughts, feelings, and experiences when you have a particularly intense emotional response to the world around you or reflecting on them at the end of each day gives you the opportunity to identify what you are actually feeling. As you journal, seek to accurately reflect everything that you are truly feeling by getting to the root of those emotions and identifying them by their true name. So, if you are feeling a sense of jealousy towards someone because they seem to fit in better than you do, make sure that you label that emotion as jealousy and not as something like anger or frustration. That way, you can honestly understand what it is that you are feeling and give that emotion the acknowledgment that it craves. You can also then look into identifying *why* you are feeling that emotion by writing down what beliefs or values you have that lead to that emotion coming up in the first place. If you are unsure, simply analyze your thoughts and see what they suggest. For example, if your thoughts were reflecting jealousy because you wanted to fit in and you felt like another person fit in with *ease*, then the belief that you have may be that fitting in with people should be easy. Because you were not experiencing ease in fitting in or you had to work so hard to defy your own personal values, you may then feel like you are bad or there is something wrong with you because it was not easy for you. In reality, it likely is easy for you to fit in, so long as you are hanging out with the right people who accurately reflect your values and beliefs. I recommend writing in this journal at least once per day so that you can begin getting a clearer understanding of your emotions, your values, and how your life may not be reflecting your values. As you begin to see this on paper, having compassion for yourself becomes a lot easier because you begin generating answers as to why you are not presently feeling like a person who is good or worthy.

Explore Your Fears and Insecurities

As you write down your emotions in your journal, chances are you will begin to generate a lot of entries that revolve around feelings of fears and insecurities. Your fears may sound silly or nonsensical in the grand scheme of things but realize that the very fact that you are feeling them makes them valid and worthy of being acknowledged and healed.

The fears and insecurities that you document, particularly if you discover that you are living largely out of alignment with your values will likely sound something like this:

- "I am afraid that I am not worthy of love."
- "No one loves me because _____."
- "If I change _____ I will have no one left."
- "I do not deserve to have my own path or way of doing things."
- "If I make a change they will not accept me."
- "I will be bullied if I act my own way."
- "My decision to go my own way could lead to eternal damnation."
- "(Your religious leader/deity) will not accept me if I honor my own values."
- "I am not allowed to be different."
- "I might die completely alone if I make any changes."

Fears and insecurities around losing the things that you have and around being unloved or unworthy of receiving love in your life if you choose to live in alignment with your own values is common. Many people who are living deeply out of alignment with their sense of self continue to live that way because they worry that if they honor their own belief or values

109

then they will lose everything. The idea of losing their loved ones, their rite to heaven or a positive afterlife (if you are religious,) their status, their home, their worthiness, or any other thing they value is enough to keep them trapped in values that do not actually serve them.

Often, these fears are developed in childhood and are never challenged or adjusted as a person grows up. Although these fears are rarely an accurate reflection of what would happen if you were to begin living in alignment with your own values, the fear still exists. Until you choose to challenge those fears and really get to the root of them and heal them, you will continue living in a state of fear and discomfort even if those fears are unfounded.

The best way to challenge your fears is to ask yourself one very simple question: "and then what?" In asking yourself this question, you allow yourself to continue playing out the scenario of what might happen if you follow your own values until you reach the point where you realize that it is unlikely that anything bad will happen.

Chapter 2: Self-Compassion

In our modern society, we are taught to apply as much pressure to ourselves as possible to attempt to get further ahead in our success. We often hear of various resources that are available surrounding the topics of "how to grow faster" or "how to achieve your goals sooner." What we rarely hear, however, is how to be compassionate with ourselves when we are not moving at the hyperspeed that society tends to dupe us into believing that we are meant to achieve. As a result, very few people truly know how to experience self-compassion when they are in a rut, struggling to advance in life, or not moving at the rapid pace that society deems as being "acceptable."

When you are unable to be compassionate with yourself, you end up putting even more pressure on yourself to achieve things that are simply not achievable within your realm of existence at that moment. Instead of being compassionate with yourself, you find yourself applying even more pressure to try and "jump start" the next level of your success or your life when, in reality, all you are doing is making yourself feel even worse. Rather than feeling motivated and ready to get into action, you end up feeling a lack of motivation and a deep inner feeling of not being good enough or worthy enough to achieve the success that you desire. In reality, your inability to move forward has nothing to do with you not being good enough or worthy enough, but everything to do with you not being compassionate enough. What you really need to be doing is showing yourself compassion, taking the time to understand why you are struggling, and equipping yourself with the tools that you need to overcome your emotions and take the next steps in your life. Sometimes, the fastest way through a hard time is to slow down and simply be compassionate with your self.

Buddhist Psychology on Self-Compassion

In Buddhism, there is a big emphasis on the importance of self-compassion and how it helps literally shift a person's mind. Buddhists often teach self-compassion through the art of meditation which is used to help people not only become more cognitively aware but also more emotionally aware of themselves. Through sitting in mindful meditation, Buddhists are able to begin bringing their emotions to the forefront of their lives and recognizing them for what they are. They may also be able to identify why that emotion exists and what message it has to offer the person engaging in the meditation. Through their Zen traditions, Buddhist teachers will educate people on the importance of self-acceptance and self-compassion. In their eyes, these two practices are essential in leading to the state of *shunyata* or emptiness.

In psychotherapy, many positive psychologists have begun researching the concepts of self-acceptance and self-compassion as well. Through studying actions like meditation and self-compassion, psychologists have discovered that one of the easiest ways to predict a person's mental wellbeing both in the present and in the future is to analyze their sense of self-acceptance. A person who accepts themselves is more likely to be compassionate towards themselves as well, meaning that they are less likely to strive to achieve standards of success that do not resonate with their true beliefs.

While self-acceptance and self-compassion have always been valued, psychologists are really starting to understand how these two states of mindfulness are really contributing to a person's overall well-being. By learning how to improve your ability to experience self-acceptance and self-compassion such as through Buddhist meditation, you are able to change your thoughts towards ones that are more positive and productive. As a result, you do not find yourself trapped in a chronic state of feeling disappointed in yourself and as though you are failing in life.

Why Self-Compassion Matters

Self-compassion is one of the most effective mental tools that you could possibly equip yourself with. When it comes to allowing yourself the opportunity to truly move forward in life, self-compassion is a key that will change everything. When you lack self-compassion, seeing yourself as a positive, worthy, good enough, and lovable human being can be extremely challenging. A lack of self-compassion can lead to you constantly striving to do more and be more because you struggle to be compassionate towards yourself when you do not reach unreasonably high standards in your life. This lack of self-compassion can lead to an obsession to become perfect which, as you likely know, is never worth pursuing since perfect truly is not an achievable standard for living.

When you inevitably fail to become the perfect person — the perfect friend, the perfect child, the perfect spouse, the perfect parent, the perfect employee, or any other role you play in your life, you end up feeling immense sadness inside. This sadness leads to you wondering what is wrong with you and why you cannot accomplish the perfect standard that you have set up for yourself. Rather than recognizing that perfect is not achievable and seeing your standard for the unreasonable expectation that it is, you end up seeing yourself as being incapable and unworthy. This type of misconception can lead to deep and painful inner feelings that ultimately lead to you not feeling capable or worthy of moving forward in your life due to an all-or-nothing view.

When you equip yourself with self-compassion, you change your point of view so that you can recognize yourself as being a human who is only capable of achieving human things in your life. Rather than attempting to hold yourself to the unattainable standards of perfectionism, you start to hold yourself to more reasonable and realistic standards that allow you to truly make progress in life. If you find yourself making a mistake or struggling with something, rather than immediately thinking that there is something wrong with you, you can instead focus on being compassionate towards yourself for your experience. Through self-compassion, you slow down, recognize your true emotions, and work through them in a loving and gentle way so that you can fully feel them and move on from them. With your challenging emotions or setbacks completely worked through and set aside, you can easily begin moving forward towards your goals again. As a result, even though you may seem like you are progressing slowly, you are actually progressing faster because you are not hitting extreme levels of burnout and overwhelm along the way. You also stop holding yourself back from your all-or-nothing attitude that leaves you feeling unwilling to begin projects for fear of not being able to accomplish them with perfection.

Benefits of Self Compassion

Self-compassion has many positive benefits that can help you achieve a better life overall. When you are compassionate towards yourself, you essentially give yourself the gentle kindness that you crave during those periods of challenge. Think of your inner emotions as a small child. When you have challenging situations that lead to feelings of not being good enough or capable enough, it is likely that your emotions are frazzled, too. Rather than feeling positive and hopeful, you likely feel fearful, angry, sad, and even embarrassed. As a small child when you felt this way, you would crave the attention of an adult who was more experienced with their emotions that would be able to comfort you and tell you that everything was going to be okay. Likewise, as an adult with challenging or festering emotions, you likely still crave that very same experience — to have someone sit with you, console you through your challenges, and let you know that everything is going to be okay. Of course, as adults, it is not exactly reasonable to believe that we are going to have someone in our lives who can offer that for us every single time we hit a challenge so we have to become that person for ourselves.

That is where the benefits of self-compassion come in. When you begin to become the compassionate, gentle, loving, and kind adult that your inner child needs, overcoming challenges in your life becomes a lot easier. Instead of attempting to whip yourself into submission through abusive acts such as bullying yourself or applying even more pressure to yourself, you instead sit with yourself and console yourself. Through that gentle act of compassion, that part of you that feels abandoned, wrong, shameful, or fearful is able to be consoled and healed. You begin to experience greater feelings of happiness and optimism and your spirit becomes more curious and adventurous. As you continue to show more compassion for yourself, your inner wisdom develops and you become more confident in your ability to have a positive impact on those around you. You experience feelings of hope and faith and your ability to make a dream and pursue that dream is improved because you become a self-starter with a purpose. Since you are no longer bullying yourself into a state of being too afraid to move or make a decision, you are able to open up and move forward with a more positive and optimistic vision of the world and how your life can look.

Becoming self-compassionate does not mean that you won't run into challenges or sometimes experience fear or uncertainty, but instead, it means that you will know how to nurture yourself through those experiences. Through this nurturing ability, you will be able to find a path forward that genuinely feels good and allows you to grow and move with ease. You will break through the chains of pessimism and self-criticism that have been holding you back and begin living with a greater sense of intention and intensity, thus allowing you to move through any challenge you may face with certainty.

Misconceptions about Self-Compassion

The modern world sees things like self-compassion as weak, ineffective, and soft. We are often taught that if we slow down and have compassion for ourselves that we must not be capable enough of moving forward through anything we face. Instead of being encouraged to have self-compassion, we are encouraged to fight harder and continue forcing ourselves forward until we truly lack any energy or will to keep fighting. Because of this conditioning, so many people do not see self-compassion as a positive, uplifting act that can truly help you. Instead, they see self-compassion as a negative, weak trait that proves that you are incapable and that something is wrong with you. This could not be further from the truth.

When you are expressing compassion for yourself, you are not showing a sign of weakness or proving that you are incapable of moving through a challenging obstacle. In fact, you are showing that you are equipped with the exact level of emotional intelligence required to move through anything. People who are self-compassionate know that by being compassionate towards themselves through challenging experiences, they can move through them with greater ease and without lasting repercussions. Through fully working through their emotions and having compassion for themselves along the way, self-compassionate people actually have a far more sustainable coping method than anyone else.

Self-compassion is also not a long-term pity party where you sit around and feel sorry for yourself and the troubles that you are experiencing in your life. When you experience self-compassion, you are not tuning out the bad things or wallowing in how troublesome your life truly is. Instead, you are actually tuning into your true emotions, acknowledging them, and processing those emotions in a complete manner. Through this completed process you are able to move on from the feelings that have you feeling incapable or unworthy and let go of them in a more complete manner, meaning that they will not linger and cause further problems in the future. As a result, you are actually using a very productive and solution-focused approach to your emotions, not one that is allowing you to simply sit around and play the victim of your own emotions.

Another common misconception about self-compassion, especially within people who experience perfectionism, is that being self-compassionate will lead to complacency. If you think that by showing yourself compassion you will be giving yourself an excuse or a pass to avoid having to make any progress in your life, you are carrying a false belief around what self-compassion truly is. Self-compassion is not intended to keep you from achieving anything in your life, if you are using it in this way then you are not using self-compassion but instead, you are using excuses. True self-compassion is not about allowing yourself to do nothing and achieve nothing. It is about being honest and realistic about what you can achieve and recognizing that your personal speed through life is plenty fast enough. You are not required to keep up with some heinous belief that you should be moving any faster than what is reasonable with you — you are allowed to move at your own pace and that is certainly enough.

A big fear that people tend to have is that if they become self-compassionate then they are somehow becoming narcissistic. This is completely untrue. Self-compassion and narcissism are entirely separate qualities and through being self-compassionate you are certainly not at risk of becoming narcissistic. True narcissism comes from an inner belief that you need to be better than everyone else around you and that you will do, say, and think anything that is required in order for you to achieve success in your life. A true narcissist is not someone who seeks to improve themselves genuinely, but rather is someone who feels a deep need to be better than everyone else as a result of a psychological disorder that causes them to see the world in a very disillusioned way. If you are self-compassionate, you are not approaching life through delusion, but instead through a highly intentional desire to actually improve yourself and experience a better life. True self-compassion is not the act of trying to be better than everyone else, it is the act of trying to be better than the person you were the day before.

Another thing that self-compassion isn't is selfish. In many scenarios, people who are expressing self-compassion are told by others that they are being selfish and inconsiderate towards those around them. For example, say that you struggle to have a positive experience at family gatherings because you tend to be treated negatively by your family. Choosing not to attend large family gatherings as an act of self-compassion would not be selfish but instead would be a positive form of self-care and self-consideration. Even though your family may attempt to bully you into thinking that you are being selfish, the reality is that you are simply being compassionate towards yourself and your needs by admitting that you do not want to sit through a negative dinner.

Lastly, self-compassion and self-esteem are not the same things. In recent years, a movement that is known as the "self-esteem movement" has risen to the surface and encouraged people to increase their self-esteem. Oddly enough, following the introduction of the self-esteem movement, narcissism increased with what is known as the "narcissism epidemic." Self-esteem is a word that measures or refers to the amount of confidence that one has in their own abilities or their amount of self-respect. On the other hand, self-compassion is the act of having compassion towards one's self. Unrelated to confidence and self-respect, self-compassion is having a sympathetic concern towards the suffering or misfortunes of yourself or others. When you have compassion for yourself, your goal is not to increase your confidence or your self-respect but instead to increase the amount of sympathy you have towards yourself and your personal experiences.

Balancing the Act of Generosity

The myth that self-compassion is selfish likely stems from the idea that people who are self-compassionate are not generous or do not give generously to others. Often times, this myth arises either from people who are no benefiting from another person in their life choosing to be self-compassionate. For example, say you have a friend who regularly asks favors of you to the point that you feel like anytime they call you, you know there is a high chance that they are only calling you to ask for a favor. In this instance, if you were to stop saying "yes" all of the time and start saying "no" because no felt like an act of self-compassion, such as if you didn't truly have the energy or the means to fulfill the favor, your friend might get angry. They may begin to feel that you are being selfish or that you are being unfair when, in reality, you are simply exercising self-compassion by not overpromising yourself to other people.

Just because you choose to be self-compassionate does not mean that you are not going to be generous anymore, it simply means that anytime you are being generous it will be an act of self-love, too. You will no longer agree or promise to do things when you truly want to say no because you recognize that it is not in your best interest when you do, so you will practice self-compassion. Because you are no longer agreeing to so many things that make you feel bad, you will not have a constant feeling of being overwhelmed by doing things that you do not want to do. As a result, the generosity that you give will be more genuine and sincere and it will not weigh you down or lead you to feel overwhelmed or under cared for. This means that you will likely be even more generous towards others, except that your giving will be more focused on doing things that also make you feel good or happy. Through this selective generosity, you will have more energy to share and give and both you and the person that you are giving to will feel positive from what you are both receiving.

In order for you to begin balancing the acts of self-compassion and generosity, you need to start identifying where your boundaries are around giving. If you have never considered this before, chances are that you are giving far more than you truly need to be. This over giving has likely lead to you feeling burnt out, used, unappreciated, or completely frustrated at least once in your life but likely many times. When you begin to address where you feel the worst during your acts of generosity, you can start setting boundaries around these acts of giving so that you no longer feel so depleted after giving to others. For example, maybe a family member constantly expects too much of you and it feels overwhelming for you to attempt to fulfill their demands. Instead of finding yourself trapped in that constant state of overwhelm and resentment, you can start setting a boundary around how much you are willing to give to that person. Maybe you will only give when you genuinely feel like you have the energy, resources, and desire to do so and in all other circumstances, you will say no. This boundary, when upheld, will ensure that you are not depleting yourself by attempting to give too much to the said family member. It will take time for you to identify your boundaries and truly uphold them but once you do, upholding your boundaries and expressing self-compassion in the act of generosity will become much easier for you. Through this act of self-compassion, you will find that giving is more heartfelt and sincere and that you do not feel obligated to give every single time someone asks for something from you.

How to Develop Your Self-Compassion

In a society that fails to truly honor the importance of self-compassion and regularly advocates for the exact opposite, you might be wondering — *"how can I become more compassionate towards myself?"* This answer is completely reasonable and justified, especially if compassion is not something that you have been taught or shown very often in your life. Below, I have outlined three steps that you can begin practicing today in order to start showing yourself more compassion throughout your life.

Practicing Forgiveness towards Yourself

If you truly want to experience the fullness of self-compassion, you need to start practicing forgiveness towards yourself. Punishing yourself for your mistakes and holding yourself in contempt for your failures will only result in you feeling even more terrified about the idea of moving forward in your life. You need to begin accepting that you are not perfect and that it is completely natural for you to experience shortcomings. Everyone has flaws and everyone goes through the process of having to accept themselves regardless of what flaws they may have had in their past, may have in their present, or may develop in their future. The reason why people value you and why you should value yourself has nothing to do with whether or not you are flawed but rather who you are as an overall person. If you genuinely lead your life with a sincere heart and a positive intention, chances are, you are a great person and you deserve to have your forgiveness surrounding the mistakes that you have made in your life no matter how big or small.

Fostering a Growth Mindset

To have a growth mindset means to be willing to focus on areas in your life where you can improve. Many people have a mindset of being "stuck in their ways" or "unable to change even if they wanted to." This mindset is not helpful when it comes to learning how to be self-compassionate as it will prevent you from developing your inner wisdom which typically coincides with developing your self-compassion. By approaching life with a sense of curiosity and a willingness to grow, you not only open yourself up to the wisdom that you need to accept yourself but you also open yourself up to the mindset that you need to accept your shortcomings. A growth mindset means that you are focused on growth, not on perfection, so the idea of failing or making a mistake becomes a lot less scary because perfectionism is not your main goal, growth is. In order to begin shifting your mindset away from perfectionism and towards growth, start focusing on quieting the voice of your inner critic. Avoid comparing yourself to others no matter who they are and start looking for people who inspire you to become a better person. Having role models who also foster a growth mindset and who already have self-compassion or who are working towards it make fostering your own growth mindset far more achievable.

Expressing Gratitude

Gratitude is a state of mind that leaves you feeling genuinely grateful for all of the blessings that you have in your life. When you are grateful, your ability to experience joy and abundance in your life is far superior to when you are not. You also teach yourself to start focusing on more positive things in life so that you can take your focus away from places like your flaws or your shortcomings. A great way to begin developing self-compassion specifically is to start expressing gratitude towards yourself on a daily basis. Each day, look in the mirror and express three to five reasons for why you are grateful for yourself. This could be anything from your willingness to continue learning and finding a way to feel better to your ability to cultivate new friendships and find a company anywhere you go. Try and choose new things every day so that you can start accumulating a list of reasons as to why you are such a great person and why you deserve to have your own sense of self-compassion.

Chapter 3: Self-Acceptance

Self-acceptance is the next step in learning how to have self-compassion. When you develop a sense of self-acceptance, you become far more willing to accept yourself as you are. As a person who features self-acceptance, you allow yourself to become more aware of your strengths and weaknesses and to remain realistic about your talents and capabilities. You also generate a deeper sense of self-worth because you begin to realize that you, like everyone else, are inherently worthy and that there is nothing you have to do in order to earn your worthiness. In other words, none of your shortcomings, flaws, mistakes, or inabilities results in you becoming worthless or undeserving. You recognize that you possess a unique set of skills and characteristics that blend together to develop a person who is certainly worthy and deserving of having and experiencing good things in life.

In this chapter, you are going to discover what self-acceptance is, how it can be achieved, and what you need to do in order to begin having self-acceptance towards yourself. A great place to start is to begin right now by accepting yourself as you are, even if that means accepting the fact that you currently struggle to accept certain aspects of yourself or your life. By having an unconditional level of self-acceptance towards yourself, you open yourself up to the opportunity to be okay with who you are. When you are okay with who you are, having compassion towards yourself for who or what you are not or for the experiences that you have becomes far easier.

The Myth of Perfection

In our childhoods, we are taught that we need to adhere to societal standards in order to be accepted, loved, appreciated, or praised by the people around us. We learn this by being celebrated and praised every time we do something great, ignored if we only do something good, or punished if we underperform. As a result, we are driven to start performing as great as we possibly can every single time we set out to accomplish something. What ends up happening is that our standards for the great increase each time as we realize that upon doing everything great so many times over, people stop praising us because they come to expect that level of greatness from us. For some people, not receiving continual praise from others is plenty because they have learned how to praise and celebrate themselves, so they simply continue achieving what feels like a high standard of greatness within themselves. For others, they crave that praise and celebration so deeply that they will continue to attempt to outperform themselves and achieve as close to perfect results as possible in order to receive positive attention. When they do not receive that positive attention, they take it as a sign that they are not doing well enough and that they need to do even better.

The perfectionism illusion is built even further in the age of social media as people post highlight reels of their lives as a way to try and market themselves as having "the good life." Many different influential marketers on social media have cultivated a presence that makes it appear like they never experience reality, but instead, they always experience a carefully crafted existence of perfection every single day. For those who find themselves continually attempting to outperform themselves as a result of perfectionism, they may find themselves attempting to replicate those highlight reels in their everyday life. As a result, they hold themselves to standards that even their role models do not hold themselves to which leads to a chronic cycle of attempting to achieve the unachievable.

The reality is, perfect is an unachievable quality that is virtually pointless to attempt to achieve. Even attempting to achieve close to perfect every single time is not ideal as it can lead to you trying to expect far too much out of yourself on a consistent basis. This does not mean that you shouldn't set your goals high or challenge yourself to do better, but it does mean that you should avoid trying to set your goals so high that they are truly unachievable. Achieving near-perfect results from time to time is reasonable and should be celebrated, but setting the expectation that you will achieve near-perfect results every time will only leave you feeling as badly as true perfectionism will.

By breaking down the myth that you have to be perfect or near-perfect at everything that you do, you give yourself the opportunity to start doing your best. You may have heard a teacher, parent, or friend's parent say this to you at some point in your childhood, "Just try your best." That is because, at the end of the day, your best truly is what matters the most as your best proves that you are challenging yourself and working as hard as you reasonably can towards doing better every time. Even minimal improvements are still something that you can celebrate in your life. You do not have to be perfect at everything or even anything in order to be accepted as a positive and worthy human. You simply have to try your best.

Allowing yourself to be Imperfect

For someone who struggles with perfectionism, you may find yourself listening the previous section while mentally disagreeing with it or attempting to justify why *your* perfectionism is different. You may attempt to barter with yourself that you are not like other people or that attempting to achieve anything less than perfect is lazy, weak, or pointless. I want you to stop right now and recognize that these very thoughts are not helpful and they will not support you in achieving self-acceptance and self-compassion. The more you attempt to justify why you are the special person that gets to be perfect while everyone else is just human, the longer you are going to hold yourself to unreasonable standards and stay trapped in a constant loop of self-disappointment.

Being imperfect does not mean that you are not going to try your best, achieve great results, or strive for excellence. It simply means that you are not going to criticize yourself to the point of self-sabotage anytime you attempt something in your life and do not achieve perfect results. When you allow yourself to be imperfect, you open yourself up to the capacity to start trying new things because you become willing to embrace the stage of being a beginner who is inexperienced. You trust that not knowing everything is okay because it simply means that you have more to learn and you trust that you have what it takes to learn *in a reasonable amount of time.* Because you have waived the pressure of being an expert on a new subject right off the bat, you give yourself the opportunity to open up to your growth mindset or the mindset of learning. Through this mindset, you equip yourself with the capacity to learn more than ever before, thus taking you directly towards the very same goal that you were so desperately attempting to achieve with perfectionism.

Unfortunately, allowing yourself to be imperfect is not always as simple as making a choice and allowing your life to transform right before your very eyes. Chances are, you are going to experience many moments of setbacks following your decision to become more accepting of who you are. You may find yourself habitually avoiding things in your life because of your fear of not doing them perfectly or you agree to do them only to find yourself fighting to achieve perfection along the way. Having these experiences is completely normal and they actually provide you with an excellent opportunity to begin practicing self-acceptance right away. You can begin by accepting the fact that you are a healing perfectionist and that you are working towards improving your habits so that you can be more self-accepting, but in the meantime, that means embracing where you are at and consciously changing. As you begin to become aware of these moments or setbacks, start by saying "I accept that I have this habit and I am consciously choosing to start changing it right now. I accept that my best is my best and I am willing to be okay with that being the best that I can offer for this." By saying something like this to yourself, you begin to accept where you are at while still aspiring to make changes and consciously choosing to do so. Remember, you cannot be perfect at breaking your perfectionism. It simply does not work like that. It is going to take time, patience, and practice as you begin to reinforce your new habit of being self-accepting no matter what your best looks like.

Making Peace with Your Past

Part of becoming more self-accepting is being willing to make peace with your past and the way that you behaved or the experiences that you had. You learned about the self and identity in Chapter 1 and now is a great time to recall the auditory self and your experiential self. Chances are the way you experience the world around you and what you are telling yourself through your inner narrator are still heavily linked to past experiences that you have had. Your perception around who you are is likely heavily shaped based on a few highlights in your past, whether they are positive or negative which means that you are probably viewing yourself in a heavily outdated and unrealistic manner.

For many people, their perception of themselves revolves largely around some of their worst experiences in the past. For example, if you were mean towards someone in your past and said something unkind out of a fit of anger and afterward you felt intense guilt around that experience, you may perceive yourself as being unkind, reactive, and mean. This could lead to you believing that you are not worthy of having nice things or being surrounded by nice people because you are too mean and therefore you are undeserving. In reality, you have probably been incredibly nice to many people throughout your life but this is the one thing that continues to play through in your mind and delude you to believing that you are not a good person. If you truly want to move forward and experience a greater sense of self-compassion and self-acceptance, you need to be willing to come to peace with these types of experiences in your life.

You need to develop a sense of trust that who you were is not who you are and that the actions you made no matter how positive or negative they may have been, do not define who you are today. In fact, they have likely never defined who you were, to begin with. Coming to terms with who you were and what you did and accepting that these are all a part of your past allows you to begin accepting yourself and the choices you have made throughout your life. When you begin to accept yourself and your choices, it becomes easier for you to decide to be okay with who you are and okay with what you have done and experienced in your life. That feeling of being okay with your past does not have to mean that you are proud of what you did or that you believe that you have to hold yourself up to the same incredibly high standards as you used to. It simply means that you are willing to accept who you were then just as much as you are willing to accept who you are now which allows you to move forward more gracefully.

If accepting your past is particularly challenging for you, you may choose to move through it at a slower and more intentional pace. Allowing yourself to become okay with just a few things at a time, based on what is relevant to your current life, and moving deeper from there as you go along may be more achievable than attempting to become okay with everything at once. In many cases, your unwillingness to accept your past will arise from a result of you still carrying unexpressed emotions around those experiences. By going through them slowly and with greater intention, you can ensure that you are giving yourself plenty of time and self-compassion to completely feel your way through each memory and move forward more completely as well.

Revisiting Bad Memories and Difficult Emotions

As you move through the process of accepting your past, there is a good chance that you are going to come across many bad memories and difficult emotions. When you arrive at these bad memories or these difficult emotions arise, you may feel an instinctive desire to shut down or avoid working through these memories so as to avoid being overcome by difficult emotions. In some cases, the pain may be too much to bear. In these circumstances, self-compassion becomes even more crucial as you need to be willing to show compassion towards yourself for the emotions that you are feeling towards these challenging memories.

Throughout the process of revisiting bad memories, it is imperative that you refrain from putting too much pressure on yourself to feel better or heal. Trust that by feeling your emotions and by having compassion for yourself, healing is happening and simply be willing to sit with yourself throughout the process. Do not put an expiration date on your feelings or put a deadline on when you want to be healed by. Just sit with yourself and be willing to slowly navigate through the healing as it happens. When you stop putting so much pressure on being healed and you start sitting with yourself as you revisit painful memories and emotions, healing happens naturally. It does not need to be pushed, forced, or sped up, it simply needs to be honored and experienced.

If you have been sitting with the pain for a while and you find that it is particularly challenging for you to sit with, you might consider moving through it more slowly. Rather than attempting to heal in one afternoon, simply allow yourself to recognize the pain and sit with it for as long as you need to before moving back into your daily living. Revisit that same memory and pain as much as you need to in order to heal it and give yourself as much time in between as you need to in order to become okay with the feelings that you have already felt along the way. By balancing the process of healing with the process of living, you ensure that you are able to continue living your day to day life while also healing the painful memories that you feel burdened by. Believe it or not, the more you are open to sitting with those challenging emotions as they come, the sooner you feel your way through them and the easier it is for you to get back to your day. Attempting to hide them, repress them, push through them faster to get them out of the way or otherwise become too controlling over your expression of your emotions will only result in them lasting longer. When you feel them as deeply and intensely as you need to, then they begin to move out faster and you are able to move on sooner.

The one thing you do need to be cautious about when it comes to challenging emotions is the unsafe expression. As you feel through your emotions, seek to do so in a safe and constructive manner. If you struggle with handling your emotions and find yourself becoming reactive or dangerous towards yourself or anyone else, it may be best to seek professional support in navigating these emotions. That way, you can release them without doing harm onto yourself or anyone else along the way.

Finding the Silver Lining of Your Past

As humans, we possess what is known as a "negativity bias" which results in us primarily focusing on the negative. This is our biological way of being able to recall bad experiences so that we could avoid experiencing them again, but it is not always effective particularly when it is unbalanced or not met with positivity. You need to learn how to balance out your mind so that you can focus on your past in a more balanced and realistic manner to avoid feeling as though your life has been one major negative experience.

The best way to begin seeing your past in a more positive light is to start by journaling all of the great things that happened to you. You should start by writing down all of the bad stories you are telling yourself and looking for the silver lining in those bad stories. For example, maybe your parents were not active in your life but you had a grandparent or an aunt or uncle who was. Maybe you got divorced when you were younger and it was particularly painful, but the beginning of the relationship was magical and magnetic. Maybe you got bullied a lot in school, but being bullied lead to you finding your best friend and to this day you two still remain close friends.

By identifying what negative stories you are telling yourself and choosing to see them as having a silver lining, you do not erase the fact that they are painful or those bad things happened. You simply choose to recognize that it wasn't *all* bad and that you did have many positive experiences throughout your life. When you start to create this sort of mental balance between the good things and the bad things that happened in your life, it becomes easier for you to see that there have been many positive elements to your existence. Accepting your past becomes a lot easier because you realize that, although it may contain a lot of pain, it also contains a lot of happiness.

Accepting Your Past and Moving On

After you have chosen to accept your past and you have decided that you are ready to begin moving forward, it is up to you to decide what that is going to look like. Until now, chances are, you have been carrying on with your life as though you are being held captive by your past choices and mistakes. This means that, in choosing to heal and accept those past choices and mistakes, you also need to choose what it is going to look like for you to move forward. In order for you to do so, you need to have positive forward-focused goals that are going to allow you to relieve yourself of the habits you carry from your unhealed self. These goals can be anything from choosing to see more positivity in your life to choosing to complain less when troubling experiences happen. You want to choose your goals based on what feels right for you and what will reflect the most positive change from your healing in a realistic manner.

When you are choosing to accept your past and move on, a great practice for you to do is to choose to wake up every single morning and forgive yourself for everything you have done in your life that has made you upset or ashamed. By forgiving yourself consciously every single day, you remember to stop holding yourself hostage for the mistakes that you have made and the way that these mistakes have impacted you. You also choose to start seeing yourself as a human who is deserving of compassion and second chances, even if you have made countless mistakes in your past.

If forgiving yourself feels challenging, start small and consider using a journal to track your forgiveness. You can easily write down what you are choosing to forgive and how that feels for you to consider forgiveness around the said topic. Be extremely honest with yourself about the feelings you have around the incident you are seeking to forgive and the blockages that have prevented you from forgiving yourself sooner. As you write these things down, the process of bringing them to your awareness and seeing them on paper will help you begin to cultivate a higher level of compassion towards yourself because you will begin to see yourself as a human with feelings. If experiencing compassion towards yourself continues to be challenging, consider how you might feel towards another person if they were to confide in you about all of the things you have just written down. Chances are, if it was coming from someone else, you would feel a lot more compassionate towards them than you may be feeling towards yourself around this very same subject. Use this understanding to begin developing compassion for yourself and to realize that you also deserve compassion for the troubles you have had in your life because you too are human.

It is critical that you realize that the process of getting to forgiveness and moving on is one that requires patience and acceptance in and of itself. Yes, the rewards of your patience and acceptance will be huge, but you will never achieve them if you do not begin practicing them right away, even if you feel as though you are not ready or worthy enough. The longer you hold onto these fallacies, the harder it is going to be for you to move forward because you will never give yourself the compassion and forgiveness that you need in order to do so. In the beginning, forgiveness may just feel like a subtle shift as you move forward in your life, but over time it will become easier and it will integrate more deeply with your begin. Forgiveness is a process and finding the capacity to begin forgiving yourself is equally as important as finding the capacity to forgive fully.

As forgiving yourself becomes easier and the forgiveness begins to sink in, living your life day in and day out becomes simpler because you are no longer living as a victim of your past. Instead, you begin to fully accept and integrate your past and let yourself off of the hook for troubling mistakes you have made along the way. As you do, leading your life from a clearer and more compassionate frame of mind becomes more achievable and thus your entire life improves because you are leading with your best foot forward.

Accepting Your Shortcomings

Every single human is born with their own perceived set of flaws that they must learn to come to terms with and accept as a part of who they are. From bodily imperfections to emotional or cognitive imperfections, every single person has something that they believe in some way makes them abnormal compared to everyone else. Even the people who seem to have it all or who behave in a way that leads you to believe that they have no flaws or difficulties are people who struggle with imperfections or who have put in a lot of time to accept themselves as they are. Not one person exists on this planet who has not had to overcome the feeling of having imperfections that result in them feeling like they are undeserving of love or goodness or like they are not valuable or worthy. Again, living in a world where social media is as largely praised as it is and people share only their highlight reels, comparing yourself to others and magnifying the intensity of your perceived flaws becomes even more dangerous. So many people believe that they are unworthy or undeserving because they look outside and only see the best in others, yet only see the worst in themselves. I am willing to bet that you have been guilty of doing this very thing in your own life too because no one is immune to this self-sabotaging behavior.

As you grow older and live with your flaws longer, you have two choices — to continue hating them and hiding for fear of being "found out" or to accept them as they are and proceed with your life anyway. If you choose the former, you will only be holding yourself back as chances are no one who truly means anything to your life or to your success will care about your flaws. If you choose the latter, you put the power of your future into your own hands and enable yourself to design your life in any way you want, regardless of what your flaws may look like or how they may impact you. People who are willing to embrace their flaws and accept them as they are, become people who are willing to grow through their challenges and overcome any obstacle that may be set in their path.

Growing accepting over your flaws whether they are physical or hidden in the inner world takes time and practice. You need to be willing to put forth an accepting and patient hand that lends you the support you need to move forward and overcomes your fears of what might happen if people "found out" about your flaws. You quite literally need to be willing to be the person who will lift yourself up so that when you reach the other side of acceptance, it is you who accept yourself and not someone else that you have become dependent on for acceptance. As you can probably imagine, this requires a lot of self-awareness, self-compassion, self-acceptance, and a willingness to be gentle with yourself as you figure out the process and find your way to success.

How you find your own self-compassion and self-acceptance will depend on what your present feelings towards yourself are and how willing to be compassionate towards yourself you are. If you are listening this book, I would imagine that you likely have a great desire to be compassionate towards yourself but realize this — desire does not equal willingness. You need to truly be willing to be unconditionally compassionate and accepting of yourself if you are ever going to make a change in your life or else changes will never truly stick with you.

Some practices you can try include getting realistic with yourself and checking your perception to make sure that you are being honest in your inner communications. For example, if you are continually telling yourself that you are ugly because you have a birthmark on your face, stop and truly consider whether this is true or not. You may not like the appearance of the birthmark, but is that because you have been taught not to love it or because you genuinely do not love it? Is your lack of love towards your perceived flaw because you have been bullied into believing that it made you unworthy, or because someone meaningful to you told you that you would be much more attractive without it? Do you genuinely believe that your birthmark or any other flaw you may possess is the real reason that you are not receiving all that you desire in life? Or is it because you are allowing it to hold you back due to a fear of being seen and truly receiving what you want from life? Maybe the problem is not your flaw, but your fear of what it might take for you to get what you desire and so you use your flaw as an excuse to hold you back.

Think about it, you were not born as a perfect human— you were born as a real human. You were born as a complete person with likes and dislikes, strengths and weaknesses, and various differences that would grow to exist between yourself and the rest of the world. All of us were born this way. Just because you are unique does not necessarily mean that you are quite as different as you may believe you are. It simply means that you are a real human just like the rest of us. Although there may be things that are different about you, there are things that are different about everyone else too. This is something we all share in common. So you see, even though it sounds unlikely, your differences actually make you pretty normal and you deserve to allow yourself to behave in whatever way feels normal to you without having to dance around your perceived flaws along the way. You can safely embrace the fullness of who you are and trust that no matter how bad they may seem, your flaws are never bad enough to result in you being unworthy of anything that life has to offer you.

Accepting Your Future Self

Believe it or not, there is a deep need for you to accept your future self just as much as you need to accept yourself as you are and accept your past as it was. If you don't, you may end up holding your future self to the same unreasonably high standards that you have just let your present and past self off of the hook for. This often happens when you heal your present and past self but fail to analyze your goals and make sure that you are being reasonable towards your future self, too. If you continue holding yourself up to goals that are beyond reasonable or dreams that are unachievable, you are only going to set yourself up for failure when you never achieve them.

Now, I'm not saying that your dreams or goals should not be challenging or that anything you truly desire to have is not achievable. After all, airplanes and hovercrafts exist, don't they? Humans really can do anything that they put their mind towards, so technically there is almost nothing that we cannot accomplish as a society or even as individual people. However, people who set big dreams and goals also realize that there is always the chance that their outcome may not look exactly as they had desired for it to look. They may discover instead that all of their efforts ended up leading them down a different path or towards a different future than they had envisioned all along. When this happens, that person can choose to feel like a constant failure because they never achieved the original dream or they can feel grateful to the original dream for giving them the encouragement that they needed to achieve their present success.

See, life will never go the way you plan for it to go, no matter how hard you attempt to stay on track with that plan. You will continually learn new things and discover new information that helps you evolve and grow as a person which means that what you are working towards will evolve and grow too. For example, say you went to school to become a behavioral psychologist and you found that you had a particular attraction towards neuroscience and the brain to the point that you preferred it over your original study of behavioral psychology. Although you may have entered school with the dream of becoming a behavioral psychologist, your introduction to the brain and its functions through those psychology classes resulted in you to realize that you were more passionate about the brain. So, if you were to go ahead and pursue neuroscience and become a brain surgeon, would that make you any less successful? No. It would simply mean that your original plan was changed by the evolution of your life and the unfolding of natural events. If you do not consciously let your future self off of the hook, you may find yourself becoming hung up on the fact that you can never see things through or that you struggle to make up your mind, rather than proud of the fact that you are a brain surgeon.

This is not restricted to large events either which may be easier for you to justify over smaller things that had seemingly less obvious or valuable outcomes than the larger shifts in your life. However, it is imperative that you realize that even the smaller evolutions matter as they are all designed to help you continue moving down a path of life that you genuinely love and that bring you sincere joy and happiness. If you do not let your future self off of the hook for changing your mind and evolving naturally, you may simply find every reason to criticize yourself for changing your mind, even though changing your mind may have been exactly the right thing to do.

A practice regularly used when it comes to accepting your future self in advance is called "releasing the outcome." In other words, you focus on setting the intention for what you desire in your life and you release the outcome by agreeing that if things work out differently than if you had planned, you will still be just as grateful and happy for your success. When you release the outcome, you are not saying that the outcome does not exist or that it is not worthy of pursuing. Instead, you are simply using your present dream and goal as your motivation to move forward and accept that it will change along the way. In this case, your dream or goal becomes a tool to help you continue moving forward and not a finite end result that allows you to determine whether or not you have been successful in your life.

Chapter 4: Silence and Self-Criticism

Most people are fairly unaware of the power that their inner critic has and how drastically it impacts their life. Many believe that the voice of their inner critic or their autobiographical self is finite and true and that everything it says is to be believed and accepted as the ultimate truth. Of course, this is not the case but we are seldom taught to see our inner critic as an untrained inner voice that truly believes it is trying to help us yet has no idea that it is going about it in the wrong way. Think of your inner critic as your overly blunt best friend — they believe they are telling you what you need to hear so that you can do better but in reality, what they say may hurt and result in you feeling unworthy and incapable. In other words, their intentions may be great but their execution is terrible which means that their approach needs to be adjusted. Just like you would with an overly blunt best friend, you need to confront your inner critic and teach it how to start treating you in a more polite and effective manner.

When you learn to master your inner critic and use it to your advantage rather than allowing it to tear you down, your inner critic becomes a powerful tool that you can enjoy in your life. Instead of holding you back or leading to your self-sabotaging behaviors, it starts propelling you forward through life and giving you the support that you need to succeed. Mastering your inner critic can also help you begin enjoying silence in your life more, as you will not spend every moment of silence being filled with the harsh echoes of your inner critic. Instead, your moments of silence will be genuinely peaceful and enjoyable and will support you in feeling even better in your life.

Turning Self-Criticism into a Gentle Supporter

Unrelenting self-criticism can be damaging and painful to endure, but not all forms of self-criticism need to be unrelenting and unmanageable. In fact, if you learn how to master your inner critic, it can become one of the gentlest yet effective supports you have in your life. The key is to discover how self-criticism truly can be mastered so that your inner critic is not running rampant and spewing hurtful criticism in your direction at any given moment. Instead, the gentle self-critic is a voice that recognizes opportunities to improve and provides you with self-awareness and understanding that allows you to begin growing in a positive manner, rather than feeling battered by your inner self. As with anything, learning how to embrace your inner self-critic and master it in a way that allows it to become gentle and supportive takes time, patience, and practice.

One way that you can begin to turn your inner self-critic into a gentle supporter is by teaching yourself to criticize behaviors instead of attributes. Unlike attributes, behavior can be changed and improved upon which means that if you are criticizing these, there is actually something that you can do about it to make things better. If you spend all of your time criticizing your attributes, you will always feel like there is nothing that you can do to have a better life because you will always be judging yourself based on things you cannot change. Learning to accept the things that you cannot change and critique and improve on the things that you can is a critical balance that is going to allow you to improve your life in massive ways.

When you are critiquing your behaviors, seek to do so in a way that is productive and effective. Realize that there is a difference between bullying yourself over a mistake and recognizing a mistake and looking for opportunities to improve upon it. If you bully yourself, you are always going to feel as though you are unable to make changes in your life because there is something inherently wrong with you or your previous mistakes mean that you are not deserving of a positive future. This is not constructive in helping you move forward and live a better life. It will only hold you back further. You need to have compassion towards yourself and offer yourself criticism in a way that allows you to actually act upon it and make changes in your life. Seek to empower yourself by pointing out your faults and offering a word of advice, rather than attempting to whip yourself into submission.

A powerful way to confront your inner critic and choose to share in a more compassionate and meaningful way is to look in the mirror and confront your inner critic and all that it has said to you. Recognize that it has always attempted to lead you down the right path and thank it for that, then get clear with yourself about how the criticizing truly feels. Do not be afraid to be honest about how it makes you feel regardless of how painful it may be to admit these feelings to yourself. Speak to your inner critic as if it were another person and be completely clear about how you feel and what you need. When you address yourself in this manner, recognizing your feelings and how damaging your current processes are becomes a lot easier because you bring the emotions and thoughts to light rather than attempting to repress them.

Going forward, each time you hear your inner critic growing harsh and abusive, slow down and remind yourself to approach your need for change in a more compassionate and mindful manner. Take the time to honestly address your feelings and what you believe you need to improve on and then make the conscious effort to begin improving upon those things. Each time you find yourself engaging in your old habit of being mean towards yourself, forgive yourself for that experience and consciously switch the vocabulary so that the criticism comes across more meaningful and polite. For example, say you feel that you struggle to communicate with others and you regularly find yourself wishing that you could share more meaningful and effective conversations with those around you. If your inner critic is unrelenting, it may begin to say things like "I am horrible at communication, I can never say the right things. I can't believe I said that. I must have sounded so stupid. I am so embarrassed about this I should not engage in conversations like this anymore. Clearly, I am incapable." This type of inner dialogue is common but as you can probably see just by reading those words off of the paper, it is mean and hurtful. If you regularly think these things, you will always think that you are incapable and that you must avoid situations where your inabilities shine through such as conversations in this situation. Naturally, conversations are unavoidable so every time you engage in one and these thoughts arise, you will only use it as further evidence that you are unworthy and incapable.

Instead, you could change the dialogue to say something more polite such as "I tried my best, but I definitely think I could have done better. When I said that, I should have been more clear and confident about what I was saying so that I was taken more seriously. I will do better next time so that I can improve on my speaking abilities and have better conversations." Not only is that a significantly more polite way of approaching yourself when it comes to criticism, but it is also done in a way that is actually constructive and supportive. When you give yourself criticism in this way, you reflect on what you felt went wrong and search for a solution immediately so that you can improve in the future. That way, you do not feel as though you are at the mercy of your inabilities because you are clearly focusing on doing better.

Activating Your Growth Mindset

Having a growth mindset means that your focus is always on looking for ways that you can improve yourself and your life. Rather than consistently staying focused on your flaws and setbacks, you focus on the things that you truly can control and then you put in every effort to improve those things. Some people naturally foster a growth mindset over the course of their lives whereas other people have to consciously focus on developing a growth mindset later in life. If you are looking to activate your growth mindset so that you can have more compassion for yourself and focus more deeply on where you can improve your life rather than obsessing over your flaws, the following strategies will help you.

View Your Challenges as Opportunities

A major component of the growth mindset is switching how you view challenges in your life. When you choose to see your challenges as a way for you to improve or move forward in your life, you literally open your mind up to a whole new world of opportunities. Rather than using excuses, victimizing yourself, or complaining every time you see a challenge arise in your life, choose to see it as an opportunity instead. Viewing your challenges as opportunities means that you take away their power to hold you back and prevent you from growing.

Each time you face a new challenge in your life, refrain from asking yourself "why is this happening to me?" and start asking yourself "what is this teaching me?" When you make this simple change in your perspective, seeing the opportunities that each obstacle presents becomes easier and you realize that you have far more options than simple defeat.

Try Learning in New Ways

There are actually four different ways of learning new information — visual, auditory, verbal, and physical. Some people need to see things in clear detail in order to understand them, whereas other people need to physically practice what they are being taught in order to make sense of the information. Everyone can learn in each of these ways but people tend to be more effective at learning in one style over the others. By discovering what learning style serves you best, you can ensure that you always tailor your learning to that style as much as you can. That way, you are far more likely to absorb what you are learning and genuinely improve your skills rather than feel defeated or like you are incapable of learning the information at hand.

Say "Learning" Instead of "Failing"

Just like you want to reframe your challenges as being opportunities, you also want to reframe your failures as lessons. When you say that something is a failure, you view it as being finite and finished, thus leading you to behave like there is no alternative to the outcome that you have received. People who believe in failure find themselves feeling as though they are always being trampled on by life and like they have no solutions to move forward and create the life that they deserve. They frequently take advantage of excuses as a way to avoid having to try again and often these people genuinely believe that their excuses provide a genuine reason as to why they cannot proceed.

If you want to find yourself regularly being held down by your setbacks and seeing every lesson as a failure, you are going to find yourself offering every excuse under the sun for why you cannot try again. In the end, you will only be robbing yourself of growth potential and preventing yourself from achieving the success that you desire. You need to reframe your failure so that you can begin seeing it as an opportunity to continue learning, rather than a finite ending to something that you deeply desire. You are not unable to move beyond failure and learn from it, you simply need to reframe how you perceive failure so that you can grow past it every single time.

Value the Process More

When you value the outcome, you end up slacking or cutting corners during the process so that you can achieve the success that you desire. What ends up happening is that your success is unsustainable because it is based on things that you do not truly know or understand. Thus, when something inevitably shakes it and you are put in a position where you need to perform, you are unable to perform effectively and everything falls apart. No one wins when you slack on the learning process and jump straight to the outcome.

Furthermore, as you already know, the outcome rarely looks the way you believe it will. If you favor the outcome more than the process, you will completely lose the joy and value in the process because you will be so fixated on what results you were planning on getting out of it. Take your time and invest in the day to day learning, it will serve you a lot more when it comes to finding value in your life and gaining genuine skills that will sustain you for the long haul.

Celebrate Your Growth with Others

Attempting to celebrate your growth on your own can become extremely lonely and fast. When it feels like you are the only one who cares about your growth and success, sometimes it can feel mildly pointless and like it may not be worth it for you to continue pursuing. That doesn't mean that you should make your growth all about receiving positive attention from other people, but inviting other people to celebrate in your growth can make it feel more meaningful and real.

When you take big steps towards celebrating new growth in your life, do not be afraid to invite those who care about you to celebrate your growth with you. Instead of holing up in your house watching a good movie by yourself, invite a good friend or even several good friends out to dinner with you. Celebrate your growth by spending time with the people that you care about and making it truly meaningful as this feels far more rewarding and special than celebrating it alone every single time.

Reward Your Actions Not Your Traits

A major drawback of living in the age of social media is that we have a tendency to see other people's traits and not necessarily their actions or behaviors. What can end up happening is that you find yourself only acknowledging your own traits and comparing them against others as well. Remember, traits or attributes are not things that you can change about yourself — they simply exist as they are.

If you want to really activate your growth mindset, focus on your behaviors and actions and reward yourself for positive behaviors. This will make it easier for you to start focusing on the parts of yourself that you can change and that when changed, can have a tremendously positive impact on your personal growth.

Care about Effort over Talent

Putting too much emphasis on your talents or the talents of others can leave you feeling incredibly judgmental over trivial things. Talent can be cultivated, meaning that anyone can become talented at anything as long as they put their mind to it and truly keep trying. This means that it is not the current level of talent that truly matters, but instead, it is the current level of effort that truly matters. People who are bound for success are going to be focusing on their efforts and putting a large amount of energy into achieving positive results from their efforts. As a result, they are more likely to succeed.

This is also a great tool to use if you are recovering from perfectionism and are working towards releasing yourself from having to get everything right from the start. When you begin to care about your own efforts more than your current level of talent, you begin to open up the energy that you need in order to achieve your desired success without putting so much pressure on yourself for not being the best right away. People who do end up achieving statuses like "the best" do not get there from trying to be perfect right away. They get there from constant, intentional effort.

Take Responsibility for Yourself

You are the only person who is responsible for everything that you have done in your life, not anyone else. Although other people may have contributed to your decisions, at the end of the day, they were not the ones who made those decisions for you, you made them. You need to realize that you are the only one who can take responsibility for yourself. When you do, making the decision to behave in a way that allows you to step out of victim mentality and into the mindset that is required for continuous growth becomes significantly easier.

Starting today, work towards taking responsibility for every single action and decision that you make. Do not let anyone else pressure you into choosing decisions that you did not truly want to make or taking actions that you truly did not want to take. When you take responsibility, you will find that it is much easier for you to then choose to take the actions that *you* want to take such as growing and improving upon yourself.

Dealing With Your Mistakes

Everyone makes mistakes. That is just a fact of life. You may have heard the saying before that goes "It doesn't matter what mistakes you make in life, what does matter is how you proceed after making those mistakes." If you make a mistake and you continually make the same mistake repeatedly, then you can guarantee that you are not actively or effectively learning the lessons that you need to in order to generate success in your life. Instead, you are staying trapped in habits and cycles that are preventing you from growing because you refuse to recognize your mistakes and make new decisions. Once again, this is another example of where taking responsibility for yourself and your life becomes valuable. When you take responsibility, you commit to taking the actions required to make a change.

Anytime you make a mistake in your life and find yourself facing results that you do not desire, commit to learning how you can move beyond those mistakes and start generating more positive results from your efforts. As you do, you will begin to find ways that you can learn and grow from your mistakes so that you do not find yourself consistently making the same ones over and over again. You can commit to finding the solution by getting yourself focused on discovering where your efforts went wrong and how you might have handled the situation differently. This allows you to dissect the mistake and see what went right and what didn't, which ensures that you are actually correcting the proper problematic behavior.

After you have discovered where the problematic behavior or action lies, you can start looking for honest solutions that allow you to improve going forward so that you do not repeatedly make the same mistakes time and again. When you give this amount of attention to improving yourself, what ends up happening is that not only do you achieve personal growth but you also achieve personal pride. Rather than feeling embarrassed, frustrated, or defeated by being trapped inside of a habit loop or a behavioral pattern, you can feel confident in your consistent improvements. This gives yourself a sense of hope that you are going to continue doing and achieving better things in life, while also allowing you to remain compassionate towards yourself when your efforts do not pay off immediately. Because you can trust in your own problem-solving abilities and your deep inner desire to change, you can trust that you are not always going to be stuck experiencing the same unwanted situations over and over again.

Aside from looking for your opportunity to improve upon your previous mistakes and making a plan to do so, you should also spend some time forgiving yourself when you have made a mistake in your life. Failure to genuinely forgive yourself can leave you feeling unresolved emotions that can result in you generating deep seeded resentment or mistrust towards yourself. Take the time to address your emotions and feel your way through the situation while also logically planning your next steps so that you can fully complete the cycle of the mistake and start stepping away from it more productively going forward.

Moving on after You've Made an Error

After you have made an error in your life, knowing how to completely move on is imperative. As you know, forgiving yourself and making a plan are two important components of moving forward because this allows you to complete the cycle and feel confident that your solution is effective enough to help you do better next time. There are other things that you should do when you are moving on from an error to help you feel a more complete sense of moving on as well, however.

One thing that you should do is communicate with anyone else who may have been affected by your error to ensure that your intentions and feelings are made clear. This also gives you the opportunity to apologize if an apology is needed which ensures that nothing is left unfinished. If you do not take the time to communicate with others and bring closure to a situation that involves other people, it can generate feelings of resentment, mistrust, and guilt. You may find that the other person struggles to trust you because you were unable to admit to your mistake and that you feel a tremendous amount of guilt around making the said mistake that leaves you embarrassed or afraid of approaching them. This can destroy relationships so bringing in an element of communication and healing any relationships that may have been damaged in the process is important. Doing so will ensure that being compassionate towards yourself is easier because you know that you did everything you could to make the situation better and you were not left feeling guilty or blaming yourself for not apologizing or correcting the situation sooner.

The next thing that you need to do is bring in an element of gratitude so that you can begin seeing the positive in your mistake. For some mistakes, seeing the positive element is going to be challenging because the mistake may have been so large and impactful that you genuinely feel as though nothing good could have possibly come from it. In these situations, look for the things that you have learned following the mistake and see how that mistake has changed your life since happening. These are all things that you can be grateful for even if the mistake itself feels like something so bad that nothing good could possibly come from it.

Anytime you make a mistake in your life, always look to see how it has changed you and how you have grown since the mistake was made. This will help you really begin adopting the growth mindset mentality of nothing being a failure because everything you endure is a lesson. When you are able to embody that mentality and begin exercising it in your real life, allowing yourself to truly grow becomes significantly easier.

Letting Go of Overthinking

The final step to overcoming self-criticism and allowing yourself to move on from mistakes that you have made in your life is to make sure that you let go of over thinking. Overthinking can result in you repeatedly going over the same experience in your head over and over again, analyzing every single aspect of the experience, and trying to find new ways to guard yourself against it. Typically, this behavior is intended to help you completely overcome behaviors that have caused you pain or brought you a discomfort in your life, but in the end, it only makes you feel worse. When you over think things, you tend to put far too much pressure on yourself to completely change your behavior in one go to avoid experiencing the same pain that your original mistake brought you. Unfortunately, no one can change all of their behaviors that quickly which will result in you only feeling worse the next time you make a similar mistake because you will feel as though you already had the perfect solution so it is your fault for performing poorly. In reality, you simply had far too high of expectations on yourself so it was virtually impossible for you to measure up to your unreasonable standards.

Not only does over thinking cause you to set unreasonable standards upon yourself, but it also causes you to spend far more time worrying and feeling bad about yourself than you need to. When you are over thinking, you keep a situation in your head far longer than it deserves to actually be there. If you are an avid overthinker, you may find yourself doing this with many different experiences and subjects which leave you feeling even worse and tremendously overwhelmed. Your brain becomes fixated on all of the ways that you believe you are underperforming in life, which can leave you struggling to find any ways that you are performing positively because you are constantly focused on your negative performance.

Simply giving up on over thinking is not always an option. If you have been over thinking for a long time or if you struggle with something like anxiety, then you may find that giving up on over thinking takes a lot of effort. Fortunately, you now know that your emphasis should be focused on the amount of effort that you have put in and not the number of results that you are getting each time. Staying focused on your efforts will ensure that you are focused on making progress which will help you truly achieve your progress in the long run.

The first step to overcoming overthinking is to start becoming aware of how big of a problem overthinking truly is for you. When you begin to practice self-awareness and become aware over how often you are over thinking and how it is making you feel, it becomes easier for you to be honest with yourself about how often you are over thinking things. Through this honesty, you can get clear and realistic on your expectations for how you can improve and what that improvement will look like over time. This way, you do not accidentally set unrealistic expectations on yourself due to a lack of truly being aware of how much your overthinking is impacting you.

Once you are clear on how much you are over thinking and have generated realistic goals on how you can overcome over thinking, you need to start equipping yourself with the necessary tools to break the habit. One great tool is to start teaching yourself to focus on what could go right rather than staying fixated on what could go wrong. While you do still want to be aware of potential problems you may face, also become aware of what positive outcomes you could experience and how they may impact your life. Becoming realistic about all of the possible outcomes including the positive ones helps you to see that every situation has many positive and negative solutions that can be derived from them. Through this, it becomes easier to stay neutral or hopeful rather than negative and fearful around what undesirable outcomes you may encounter along the way.

Another way to begin overcoming over thinking is to break the cycle through distractions. When you distract yourself into being happier, your brain learns to start breaking down the cycles that lead to overthinking and literally wires itself into having new habits instead. You can easily distract yourself from over thinking through using positive affirmations, enjoyable hobbies or activities, exercise, or trying something new or different from your usual activities. By breaking out of your normal routine or putting your focus on something more productive, your brain is forced to pay attention which results in you no longer overthinking.

Sometimes overthinking stems from not giving yourself enough time to adequately assess each situation that you are entering. If you are someone who regularly jumps into situations without much thought, or if you used to be like that and you have experienced a tremendous number of unwanted outcomes, you may be afraid to take leaps in your current life. As a result, you may rely on things like overthinking to help you avoid making a significant mistake in the future. What ends up happening, however, is that you find yourself trapped in "analysis paralysis" or in a state where you are unable to stay focused or make a move because you are so afraid of failing. In this circumstance, exercising boundaries is imperative as it will support you in having adequate time to assess your situation and make decisions without feeling pressured to act immediately. For over thinking specifically, set a timer for five minutes analyzing everything that you are afraid of and allowing yourself to think through all of the thoughts that are keeping you worried. Then, set it again for ten minutes so that you can write everything down and get it out of your mind, thus preventing you from feeling as though you have to continually think it in order to avoid "forgetting" about your chosen solution. Once you are done journaling, commit to letting go of the situation and move forward using a tool such as distraction to help you fully disengage from your worry and take actionable steps forward.

Lastly, many people will engage in overthinking as a way to make up for what they feel was a poor performance on their behalf. They believe that by over thinking about the situation and identifying every improvement that they could have possibly made then, in some way, they have retroactively improved their performance and made up for their mistakes. In reality, this is not true. No amount of thinking about alternative outcomes will change the way that the situation unfolded. The best thing that you can do is try your best in every single situation and then pick one or two things you might improve on going forward so that you can have a more positive impact. By staying honest with yourself about how much effort you put in and reasonable with yourself about how much you expect to improve going forward, you can break the cycle of chronic over thinking and move forward positively.

Chapter 5: Mindfulness and Self-Awareness

The final step in fostering a stronger sense of self-compassion is developing your mindfulness and self-awareness. When you develop mindfulness and self-awareness, you equip yourself with the two most important tools required when it comes to improving your relationship with yourself and having a deeper sense of compassion and sympathy towards yourself going forward. People who are more mindful and self-aware have an easier time identifying their self-sabotaging behaviors, putting them into perspective, and moving past them in a productive manner.

In this final chapter, you are going to discover how you can begin building your mindfulness and self-awareness practices in a way that will genuinely support you in feeling a deeper and more meaningful sense of self-compassion. You should seek to implement these practices on a daily basis to ensure that you are always putting in the effort to have a more positive relationship with yourself. As with any relationship in your life, the more genuine attention and care you give to your relationship with yourself, the more you are going to get out of it. Since this is such a personal experience which means that you will experience a greater sense of joy, optimism, self-worth, and self-confidence around your ability to grow and become a better version of yourself every day.

As you go about implementing these practices, remember to embrace deep self-acceptance along the way. Your relationship with yourself may not be where you want it to be right now which may leave you feeling a variety of different emotions such as sadness, pain, anger, and grief. Be patient with these feelings and accept them as they arise so that you can work through them and improve your life going forward.

Practicing Presence

Presence allows you to become more grounded in your current moment and enjoy it for what it is. When you practice presence, you are able to let go of all of your regrets from the past and all of your worries for the future so that you can enjoy the present moment to the fullest of your ability. Through becoming more centered and present, you give yourself the gift of feeling less mental worry and a greater capacity to genuinely receive moments that bring you joy, happiness, and contentment.

Developing your presence is going to require you to deny everything you have ever learned about the getup and go of modern living and start focusing on how you can start slowing down and really embracing each moment as it comes. Instead of constantly checking your calendar or clock for indication of it being time to move onto the next activity, slow down and allow your self to fully immerse into the current one for as long as it lasts. You can do this by setting regular breaks for yourself and committing to completely releasing any unwanted thoughts from your psyche during those breaks, such as thoughts that have you focusing on what comes next or what needs to get done. Once you have released those thoughts, bask in the silence of the moment and start to become aware of what is going on around you right now in the present moment. As you read this even, slow down and take a break so that you can become present in your experience. Notice what is around you, listen to the sounds going on in your environment, and pay attention to any feelings you may be having right now. Getting actively engaged at the moment brings you out of your thoughts and into the experience so that you can start freeing up mental space and enjoying your life more fully.

If you find that you are the type of person who constantly doubles, triple, and quadruple check your watch or phone for an indication that it is time for you to move on to the next activity, look for a more productive way to manage your time. Rather than constantly feeling a nagging to check the time, set

155

an alarm or a reminder that will go off a few minutes before you need to switch activities. This way, you can completely let go of the need to check the time over and over again and start focusing on being present. Instead of the constant distraction, you can trust that you are going to be informed of your next activity with plenty of time without you having to personally pay attention to the time itself.

Lastly, developing a meditation practice is a great way for you to practice releasing your busy mindset habits and start focusing on the present moment. When you develop a meditation practice you give yourself the opportunity to intentionally slow down and practice presence through your meditation. Research suggests that just 10 minutes of meditating each day, ideally in the morning, will support you in having a greater ability to feel more at peace while also staying more present from moment to moment.

Feeling Deeply and Moving On Completely

A highly valuable practice you can use to start developing a deeper sense of mindfulness and self-awareness is to start allowing yourself to deeply feel before moving on completely. In many instances, we find ourselves feeling busy, rushed, and disengaged from every situation that we encounter because we are struggling to fully feel every experience that we have in our lives. When you struggle to feel things deeply, your mind attempts to hold on to those memories and emotions so that you can revisit them at a later time. When you never give yourself that later time, you find yourself holding on to too many things inside of you so you struggle to fully sink into each moment and emotion which keeps you in the cycle of never fully feeling and releasing.

In order to help you deepen your presence and have better experiences in life, begin fostering the art of feeling deeply and releasing completely. Each time you engage in a new moment or feel a new emotion arise, allow it to completely wash over you and feel it to the very depths of what it is. This does not necessarily mean that you need to act on every single emotion to the maximum extent that you can. Instead, just focus on acknowledging it and how far it goes and allow it to really sink into your heart and body as a true and genuine emotion that you are experiencing. If you are in a place where it is safe to do so, do not be afraid to let your emotions out completely by crying, yelling, punching a pillow, or simply lying down and feeling the despair wash through you. Once you have completely felt the depths of the emotion, allow it to be released completely. Since you have felt it completely, releasing it completely is easier because there is nothing residing within you that keeps you attached to that emotion.

If you do find that you are somewhere that seems unacceptable for you to release your emotions such as at work or in an important meeting, give yourself permission to file them away for later. When you do, always make sure that you come back to that emotion as soon as it is reasonable for you to do so and feel into it completely so that you can also release it completely. By setting the intention to dig into and feel that emotion all the way, you ensure that it does not fester and result in you experiencing it any more than you need to.

The Value of Daily Reminders

As you go about changing your habits to incorporate for more mindfulness and self-awareness, nothing will prove to be more valuable than the very simple tool of daily reminders. Having daily reminders in your life to support you in remembering to engage in a mindfulness practice or become aware over your present state of being can support you in actually remembering to engage in and reinforce your new positive habits. The more you see your reminders and engage in your mindfulness and self-awareness, the easier it will be for you to start reminding yourself to engage in these behaviors as well. Over time, you will find that your inner ability to remember and then actually fully engage will improve, allowing you to experience more joy and positivity from your life.

There are many ways that you can set daily reminders for yourself so that you actually pay attention and listen to them. The best way is to set daily reminders in a variety of different ways so that you are actually paying attention and following those reminders as seeing the exact same reminder too often may lead to you ignoring it. You can set reminders on your phone to periodically remind you throughout the day, leave post-it notes around your home and office, and even write it down in your calendar.

Another creative way to remind yourself to engage in mindfulness is to set triggers that are meant to help remind you spontaneously. For example, maybe you decide that from now on every single time you see the color orange you are going to pause for a moment and begin practicing mindfulness and self-awareness. By setting triggers like this, you ensure that you are going to practice mindfulness at all times and not just when you see the reminder on your phone go off or the note in your day timer each morning.

The more reminders you set and the more you commit to actually acting on those reminders, the easier it will be for you to get the fullest value out of them. Over time, you will become so used to these reminders that you will naturally begin engaging in mindfulness and self-awareness all on your own. Any time you notice an intense wave of emotion or a challenging situation surface before you, you will slow down and tap into your mindfulness and self-awareness practices so that you can begin feeling more positive overall. This will continue to develop as you continue to improve your growth mindset which will ultimately lead to you experiencing a continually more positive life experience overall.

Meditation for Mindfulness and Self-Reflection

There are many meditations that you can practice for mindfulness and self-reflection, including the two following ones that I have provided for you. The first one is a shorter meditation that you can practice on the go any time you find yourself feeling intense emotions or energies rushing through your body and find yourself needing to check in with yourself. The second is longer and gives you a more intentional and meaningful connection with yourself so that you can really tune into your inner feelings and process them more effectively. You should seek to use each of these daily, as they will both provide you with great value in improving your overall mindfulness and self-awareness and help you to feel a deeper sense of peace and calm in your life.

A Quick Breathing Meditation

In order to practice this quick breathing meditation, you simply need 2-3 minutes of personal time and a willingness to tune in and fully listen during that period of time. Then, all you need to do is sit or stand somewhere that you will not be distracted and straighten out your posture. Focus on elongating your back, dropping your shoulders, letting your tongue muscles relax, relaxing your core, and fully embracing a moment of peace. When you have completely relaxed your body, take a few deep breaths in and out, counting to four with each inhalation and counting to four with each exhalation, aiming to take at least ten complete breaths.

After you have taken your breaths, ask yourself "How am I feeling right now?" and "What do I need right now?" Listen to the answers that arise so that you can get a clear sense of what emotions arise for you and what needs you may have that are not presently being met. Then, completely acknowledge your emotions and your needs and create a plan to feel through your emotions and fulfill your needs as soon as you possibly can. By acknowledging what you are feeling and what you need and creating a plan to address these two things, you assure yourself that there is no need to worry or feel neglected because you are actively seeking to improve your present conditions.

If you are in a moment where you can actively feel through your emotions or meet your needs, do so right away. If you aren't, be very diligent about coming back to your emotions and needs at a later time and fulfilling them completely as this will allow you to begin developing a sense of trust in yourself and your ability to take care of yourself completely.

A Full Body Scan Meditation

The full body scan meditation is one that you should attempt to accomplish on a daily basis. One great body scan every day, ideally at night time, is a great opportunity for you to check in with yourself, get a sense of what is going on within your mind, and tap into any emotions or thoughts that may be unresolved from the previous day. Consider this as your opportunity to show yourself compassion on purpose particularly if you have been having troubles showing compassion for yourself throughout the day. As you begin to give yourself this quality time and pay attention to yourself on a more consistent basis, you will find that you begin cultivating a deeper relationship with yourself that allows you to tune in even more.

To begin your body scan, simply begin by sitting or lying down and taking several deep breaths into your diaphragm. Fill up your lungs as completely as possible, allowing yourself to relax into each breath as you take it for as long as possible. Once you feel yourself entering a state of relaxation, begin drawing your awareness into your body and seeing if you notice any specific areas that are filled with tension. If you do, go through those areas one by one and make a conscious effort to relax them completely before you begin with your official body scan.

With your body completely relaxed, go ahead and draw your consciousness into your feet and take a moment to notice if you are carrying any tension in them before intentionally relaxing them completely. Then, draw your awareness up into your shins and consciously become aware of any tension you may be carrying there and release it completely, too. Continue doing this all the way up your body by drawing your awareness to your knees, thighs, glutes, hips, abdomen and lower back, torso, middle back, chest and upper back, shoulders, biceps, forearms, hands, neck, and head. By consciously drawing awareness into each of your body parts and letting that awareness rise up through you, you give yourself the opportunity to intentionally release any stress that you may be carrying within your body. This is known as a complete body scan or a form of progressive muscle relaxation that allows you to completely de-stress your entire body and release anything that you may be carrying within you. Once you are done, be sure to address any feelings that may have come up along the way and allow yourself to completely process them and then release them so that you are capable of moving forward completely.

Mindfulness Exercises for You to Try

In addition to meditation, there are many other mindfulness practices that you can try to help you enter a deeper state of mindfulness and self-awareness. These practices range from things that you can actively use to make yourself more consciously aware during your day to day experiences or that you can engage in during your personal time to improve your mindfulness.

Spontaneous Environmental Check In

A spontaneous environmental check-in is a simple practice whereby you slow down and pay attention to the environment around you as you engage in any form of day to day experience. You can do this anytime you notice that you are checking out or struggling to stay grounded in the moment or simply to see just how tuned in you really are. This can be done at work, when you are spending time with friends, or even when you first open your eyes in the morning. The more you practice it, the more mindful you will become.

In order to practice your spontaneous environmental check-in, you simply need to tune into your environment and notice at least one thing that is stimulating each of your senses. So, you want to notice one thing that you see, one thing that you hear, one thing that you feel, one thing that you smell, and one thing that you taste. Since you are likely not tasting your environment at all times, taking a sip of water or chewing a stick of gum is a great way to engage your sense of taste during experiences where you are not actively eating or drinking something as a part of your experience.

Mindful Listening Practices

Listening is a powerful tool that can help you really plug into your environment. A great listening practice that can be done in your personal time is called mindful listening and it requires you to use a piece of music or composure to help you engage in mindful listening. The goal as you listen to this music is to listen to each word and actively let each word go as you move onto the next word in the song. Rather than attempting to remember what has been said or formulate an opinion or understanding around what the song means, simply listen to it and experience it in complete presence.

Focusing On Your Details

If you are struggling to stay present or mindful during any particular experience, practice focusing intently on your details. In order to do so, simply bring your awareness into the details of what you are doing. For example, if you are washing dishes, pay attention to the temperature of the water, the texture of the soap, and the visual of watching the dish become clean. Allow yourself to pay close attention to each step of the process and really immerse yourself into how it feels for you so that you can get deeply engaged in the process. By really embracing each detail of the process, you encourage your mind to stay focused on what you are doing rather than allowing it to grow bored and get distracted by other things that may be going on around you.

Self-Reflection Exercises for You to Try

Self-reflection is a great opportunity for you to improve your self-awareness and develop a deeper understanding around who you are and what you have to offer. Practicing self-reflection on a daily basis gives you the opportunity to both understand yourself on a deeper level and decide what you may wish to improve upon in your life so that you can experience greater results from your self-improvement efforts. You should seek to engage in at least one self-reflection exercise per day so that you can really immerse yourself into your growth and learning, as well as cultivate a strong relationship with yourself.

Self-Reflection Journaling

Nothing beats a good old fashioned journal when it comes to learning how to improve upon yourself and become the best version of yourself that you possibly can. Self-reflection journaling is an easy activity that you can engage in on a daily basis so that you can pay attention to how you are doing and really dig into areas of your life that you want to improve on.
The best way to utilize your self-reflection journal is to write down all of the things that you wish you had done better in your day and all of the things that you are exceptionally proud of. For the things that you wish you had done better, write about why you wish you had done better and how you wish you had done things differently. That way, you have an idea of what you can do in the future as well as a clear understanding as to why it happened so that you can practice true compassion with yourself. For the things that you are proud of, celebrate yourself and take a moment to deeply immerse into your pride around these subjects.

Listening In On Your Self-Talk

Eavesdropping on your self-talk is a great way to listen to how you are communicating with yourself and get a better idea on how you can improve the way that you are speaking to yourself. When you listen in on your self-talk, you can get clear on how it may be helping or hindering your success in life. If your self-talk is compassionate and caring, then chances are you are engaging in positive self-talk that is actually supporting you in moving forward in life. However, if your self-talk sounds harsh or condescending, you can easily regain control over it and move back into a state of deeper compassion so that you are no longer attempting to bully yourself into submission.

Tracking Your Progress

The best way to track your progress when it comes to personal development, especially around things like mindfulness and self-awareness which tends to be challenging to measure is through snapshot journaling. Snapshot journaling essentially requires you to write one journal entry per week where you get very honest about how you are currently embracing mindfulness and self-awareness in your life. Be very clear about how well you think you are doing and make sure to highlight any areas where you feel that you are not performing as well as you believe you could be.

By honestly capturing how you are feeling in regards to mindfulness and self-awareness or any other aspects of yourself that you are trying to improve on, you give yourself clear progress notes to look back on. You can then read back through your snapshots and see just how much you have changed and how far you have come based on the notes you have taken. Of course, based on the nature of how this works, you will only get incredible results if you stay highly honest with yourself and truly capture the reality of how you are doing each time.

Another way that you can track your progress is to communicate with a loved one who knows you well. By asking for feedback and requesting them to reflect on your growth as far as they have seen, you also give yourself the opportunity to get a clear understanding of your persona and how it may be reflecting your personal improvements. Be sure not to ask too often or it may become overwhelming or ineffective, but do not be afraid to ask from time to time just to get a clear understanding of how far you have come and where you may need to improve on going forward.

Conclusion

Congratulations on seeing your own personal journey of *Self-Compassion* all the way through until now! While I know your personal journey with cultivating self-compassion will never truly come to an end, our journey together for this book is. Before you go, however, I want to make sure that you truly feel equipped with all of the tools that you need to completely embrace your new skill of self-compassion.

First, I want you to recall the importance of your relationship with yourself and the reality of how your identity is created between three states of awareness that we all possess. I hope that in learning this concept that you were able to develop a stronger understanding of how your perception of who you are and who you truly are will never fully line up. Likewise, how other people see you and who you truly are will never fully line up, either. You are a human with many qualities, characteristics, and aspects to your identity, each of which extends far beyond any one person's perception.

By realizing that your identity is far larger than what you or anyone else thinks of you, I hope you understand how to develop a deeper sense of self-compassion by recognizing that you are not able to be chalked up to any one label. You are by no means incapable, worthless, mean, pathetic, useless, or any other labels that you may be cruelly identifying yourself against. Likewise, you are not any one positive label. In fact, you are many things and in many different ways and who you are change depending on who you are around and what persona you are embracing at that moment. Although there are many constants in who you are, there are also many evolving pieces of your identity that contribute to the reason as to why "who" you are is such a challenging thing to summarize.

When you stop trying to identify yourself as any one thing and you open your mind up to the concept that you are many things and nothing all at the same time, it becomes easier for you to stop attaching yourself to labels. In that, you give yourself the freedom you require to begin developing a deeper and gentler connection with yourself and all aspects of your inner identity. The more you detach from labels and the belief that you are one finite identity, the more you will find yourself feeling the freedom to love yourself deeply and intensely.

The second thing I want you to take away from this book is that your self-compassion is something that will evolve over time so do not worry if you have reached this point and you do not yet feel a deep sense of compassion for yourself. The more you practice the tools that I have provided you with here in this book, the more you are going to feel a deeper sense of compassion towards yourself. At first, that sense of compassion may barely crack through the surface of everything that you are feeling and the shell that you keep yourself protected by. However, the more you practice, the deeper your compassion towards yourself will become and the easier it will be for you to hold space for yourself and accept yourself as you really are.

Always be willing to accept yourself for where you are at in your journey and have faith that you will improve as you move forward. Remember, it is okay not to be okay and it is okay to feel like you are not where you wish you were in life. If you feel frustrated, sad, or defeated because you are not further ahead in life, that is okay. Accept yourself as you are and for the emotions you have around what you are going through each day and through that acceptance, it will feel easier for you to heal and move forward.

Lastly, if you enjoyed this book I ask that you please take the time to review it on Audible.com. Your honest feedback would be greatly appreciated. Thank you.

Now, I would like to share with you a free sneak peek to another one of my books that I think you will really enjoy. The book is called "Guided Meditation for Stress and Anxiety Relief" Published by PMT Publishing and it's A Practical Guide To Improve Sleep And Relaxation Using: Self Healing, Awareness of Breath, Mindful Body, Visualization and Imagery, and also Breathing Exercises

Enjoy!

Guided Meditation for Relaxation

The Following scripts will truly take away all the stress that you are experiencing on your everyday lives those stress if taken for granted can lead to various mental disorders such as depression and anxiety.

By practicing these guided meditation scripts for relaxation you are doing something good for yourself specifically your overall wellness. Right now we will be doing a session of guided meditation for relaxation using these following scripts.

Script #1

- Find yourself a peaceful place to sit. Turn off your phone and also other gadgets as they are also a form of distraction.
- Dim the lights because this is the point in time for optimal relaxation and inner peacefulness.
- Take a moment to make sure that you are warm enough, and that you are seated at ease. Rest your hands freely in your lap.
- Now close your eyes.
- Take a lengthy but slow, deep breath in...hold it for two to three seconds, and then slowly exhale.
- Just allow any stress to dissolve away as you slowly relax more and more deeply with each breath.
- Take another long slow, deep breath in...hold it, and then exhale. Empty your lungs completely with your out-breath.
- Take a third deep inhale, just take your time.
- Hold it for a moment, and then release it.
- Right now you are beginning to undergo into a state of deep relaxation.

- Continue to breathe gradually and softly
- Relax.
- Now bring your awareness to the top of your head.
- Visualize a feeling of relaxation beginning to spread down from the topmost portion of your head.
- Let the muscles in your forehead and temples relax.
- Allow your eyes to relax.
- Let your cheeks and jaw soften and release all the tension.
- Now this peaceful feeling flows down your neck and deep into the muscles in your shoulders that soothes and releasing them.
- Then inhale and exhale normally.
- Allow this peaceful feeling to flow through your arms.
- Relaxing and soothing...all the way to the tips of your fingers.
- As your body relaxes your mind and thought relaxes and eventually becomes featherweight, like wisps of clouds on the breeze.
- Now the calm feeling streams through your chest and your stomach.
- Sense how this area gently rises and falls as you breathe gradually and deeply.
- So soothing and relaxing...
- Turn your concentration to your back, and experience this relaxing feeling surge all the way down your spine.
- Now the serene feeling streams through your lower body.
- Relax your buttocks and then the back of your thighs as well as the front of your thighs.
- Experience all these huge and strong muscles becoming wobbly and relaxed.

- The relaxing feeling streams down through your knees, and into your calves.
- Your ankles are relaxed, as well as your feet relax.
- Your whole body is soft, calm and relaxed.
- Now it is time to depart the external world at the back and go on an inner journey.
- A journey to a place of deep inner peacefulness.

Script #2
- Visualize that you are standing on a white sandy beach.
- It's early in the morning, and a light, hazy fog surrounds you.
- The sun is rising gradually. You can feel the humid, orange sun rays on your face and your body.
- You are feeling satisfied and at ease leaving you with a truly relaxing sensation.
- The sand beneath your bare feet is soft and warm.
- A light breeze touches your face.
- This beach is empty because of that you are all alone and you have all the time in the world.
- Listen to the soothing sound of the ocean. Its waves are moving gently on the shore.
- Start to walk lightly through the fog towards the water.
- A little boat is waiting for you. The boat is comfy and steady.
- Observe that it is tied to the shore with a sturdy rope.
- Walk to the corner of water and step into the boat.
- You are experiencing a very peaceful feeling, completely safe, and completely relaxed.
- When you are all set, loosen the rope and let it go.
- Unwind, and allow the natural waves of the ocean to direct you away from the beach.

- Your boat moves smoothly. It collides ever so gently in the water. This motion soothes you even more deeply.
- The sun is now elevated in the sky. Its light has accumulated power.
- Observe that the fog that surrounds you is starting to evaporate.
- You can see the air becoming more lucid.
- Stare at as the sun's rays melt all of the fog. Now you can see clearly in all directions. It is as though a covering has been lifted.
- Radiant ocean water bounds you on all sides, and in front of you, a tiny island comes into view.
- Your boat moves nearer to the island, sliding gradually and effortlessly through the water.
- The island is soaked in sunlight. It is sheltered in tropical palm trees that swing smoothly in the breeze.
- Your boat moves gradually forward and comes to rest on the shore.
- You have reached your destination.
- Move out of the boat and take a minute to be grateful for this place of magnificent beauty.
- Beautiful birds dance from and transfer from one tree to another, and brightly colored flowers grow in great quantity.
- The air itself seems to sparkle and moves with pure and luminous energy.
- You can hear the relaxing echo of the wind as it passes through the trees.
- In this place, you are free from all memoirs of the past. You are free from all worries about the future and you are free from all tasks.
- This is a place of complete peace, and it is all yours.

- Observe a gap among the palm trees. In the middle of this opening, there is a narrow path that leads deep into an abundant green forest.
- Start your journey into the center of the forest. Follow the path as you wander among columns of ancient trees.
- This forest seems well-known to you, like the memory of a pleasant dream, or a place you visited as a child.
- Walk deeper into the forest. You are directed by a force that you trust, and that makes you feel secure, cherished, and tranquil.
- You have arrived at the very heart of the forest. Prior to you is a sparkling river of crystal clear water.
- A river of perfect tranquility, the river is round and it tops with pure spring water.
- Notice that the water is perfectly still, reflects, and free from any little ripple.
- A ladder with three steps pathway down into the water, you make your mind up to bathe in this supernatural river, and you undress.
- As you take the first dip into the river, you notice that the wind has eased. All the trees have become stationary.
- As each moment passes, the world around you becomes calmer and calmer every second, and you yourself become more and more tranquil.
- As you lower yourself onto the next step, all the birds in the forest become quiet.
- Your mind succumbs to peace because of the complete silence of the place.
- Now lower yourself onto the next and concluding step and slide into the water.
- Feel yourself sliding into a deep state of relaxation. In this river, your thoughts simply dissolve away.

- All is peaceful and silent. The only sound that left is the noise that is coming from the waves, far off in the distance.
- Your mind seems to spread out because of this you feel the infinite relaxation of the surroundings.
- For the next few minutes, enjoy this occurrence of isolation and inner peace.
- When thoughts arise, simply release and bring back to your awareness of the noise of the waves. When it is time to go back home I will guide you the pathway to your home.

Guided Imagery

The practice of guided imagery is very moveable, as it relies on nothing more than a person's visualization and concentration abilities which people always possess.

But, like most techniques requiring mental awareness, it is usually most successfully practiced with no distraction in a setting that is liberated from distracting stimulation. Even the toilet can be used in a pinch if no other suitably private and peaceful location is available.

- There is no one accurate way to use visual imagery for stress relief. However, something alike to the subsequent steps is often recommended. So let us start here is a quick session of guided imagery for relaxation.

- Find a place where there are people other than you. It must be a peaceful space and find a comfortable spot there for you.
- Take a few gradual and deep breaths to center your attention and calm yourself.
- Now, close your eyes.
- Visualize yourself in a gorgeous place, where everything is as you would perfectly have it.

- Some people visualize a beach, a mountain, a forest, or a being in a favorite room sitting on a favorite chair.
- Visualize yourself becoming calm and relaxed. Otherwise, imagine you smiling, feeling happy and having a good time.
- Concentrate on the different sensory qualities that can be found in your scene so as to make it more vivid in your mind. For instance, if you are imagining the beach, use up some time vividly visualizing the warmth of the sun's rays on your skin, the smell of the ocean, and the sound of the waves. The more you can appeal to your senses, the more vivid the entire image will become.
- Stay put within your scene, touring its different sensory features for five to ten minutes or until you feel relaxed.
- While relaxed, assure yourself that you can return to this place whenever you want or need to relax.
- Open your eyes again and then you are now back to the reality relaxed and more peaceful.

Meditation Exercises for Relaxation

Progressive Body Relaxation - guides to deep relaxation of both the body and the mind. It is said that 15 minutes of this meditation relaxation exercises may leave you feeling refreshed more than hours of sleep!

So if you are feeling stressed and tired and you still have things to finish, practice this relaxation and you will find that it rejuvenates the body and gives you clarity and peace of mind. And of course, it is a nice way to drift off into a deep and peaceful sleep as well as a better presence of mind.

- Lie down at ease on your back, support your head with a cushion if you require to and if your back is uncomfortable place a pillow beneath your knees.

- Make your body warm by covering it with a towel or blanket. Let your arms roll away from your body and split your legs a little bit, letting your feet fall outward.
- Be mindful of your breath and give it a privilege to slow down and deepen. If your mind becomes preoccupied just draw it back naturally to your breathing.

- You will be putting your attention on a particular area of your body and soothing it by feeling it expand on the inhaling and relax on the exhaling.
- Soothe your body by putting one breath in each of the following areas:
  - ✓ Toes
  - ✓ Heels
  - ✓ Feet
  - ✓ Ankles
  - ✓ Calves
  - ✓ Knees
  - ✓ Thighs
  - ✓ Hips
  - ✓ Lower back
  - ✓ Middle back
  - ✓ Upper back
  - ✓ Shoulders
  - ✓ Upper arms
  - ✓ Lower arms
  - ✓ Wrists
  - ✓ Hands
  - ✓ Palms
  - ✓ Neck
  - ✓ Throat
  - ✓ Face
  - ✓ Lips
  - ✓ Cheeks
  - ✓ Eyebrows
  - ✓ Forehead

Awareness of Breath

This guided meditation on the breath will help you release stress and anxiety. Ready yourself to be acquainted from the normal mode of doing a task to a mode of non-doing anything at all.

Procedure:

- Sitting in an erect posture, either on a straight back chair or on a cushion.
- As you allow your body to become still, bring your attention to the fact that you are breathing and become aware of the motion of your breath as it comes into your body and as it leaves your body.
- Not maneuvering the breath in any way or trying to alter it. Simply being aware of it and of the feelings associated with breathing and observing the motion of air deep down in your belly.
- Feel the abdomen as it expands gently on the inhalation, and as it falls back towards your spine on the exhalation. Being totally here in each moment with each breath.
- Not trying to do anything, not trying to get any place, simply being with your breath.
- Giving full care and attention to each inhalation and to each exhalation. As they go after the other in a cycle that never ends and flow. You will see that from time to time your mind will wander off into thoughts.
- When you see that your mind is no longer here, no longer with your breathing, and without judging yourself, bring your attention back to your breathing and traverse the waves of your breathing. You must be fully conscious of the duration of each breath from time to time.

- Every time you discover your mind wandering off the breath, gently bring it back to the present which is back to the time to time observation of the flow of your breathing.
- Use your breath as a medium to focus your attention, in order for you to bring you back to the present whenever you notice that your mind is becoming preoccupied with thoughts.
- You can also use your breath to tune into a state of relaxed awareness and peacefulness.
- Now as you observe your breathing, you may find from time to time that you are becoming aware of sensations in your body.
- As you uphold consciousness of your breathing, see if it is possible to increase the scope of your consciousness so that it includes a sense of your body as a whole as you sit here.
- Feel your body, from head to toe, and become aware of all the sensations in your body. So that now you are observing not only the flow of breathing but the sense of your body as a whole.
- Being here with whatever feelings and sensations come up at any moment without judging them and without responding to them, just being fully here and conscious.
- Keep yourself away from any distractions with whatever your feelings are and with your breath and a sense of your body as a whole and again whenever you observe that your mind wandering off, just return it back to your breathing and your body as you sit here and not going anywhere as well as not doing anything just simply sitting quietly.
- Restore your consciousness on the body as a whole and on the breath as it inhales and exhales out of your body.
- Come back to a sense of fullness of each inhales, and the fullness of each exhales. If you find yourself at any point drawn into a flow of thinking and you see that you are no longer mindful of your breath, just using your

breathing and the feeling of your body to secure you and calm you in the present.

- Just being one with your breathing from time to time, just sitting in tranquility, and looking for nothing at all. Just as it observes it unfolds. Just being right here and right now you realized that you have the unity of your body.
- As the session concludes, you might give yourself some credit for having spent this time nourishing yourself in a different way by dwelling in this state of not doing anything.

If you enjoyed this preview of my book "Guided Meditation for Stress and Anxiety Relief", be sure to check out the full book on amazon.com

Thank you.

CPSIA information can be obtained
at www.ICGtesting.com
Printed in the USA
BVHW071118130819

555664BV00002B/308/P